In Hiding

THE AZRIELI SERIES OF HOLOCAUST SURVIVOR MEMOIRS: PREVIOUSLY PUBLISHED TITLES

In Hiding

Marguerite Élias Quddus

A memoir illustrated by the author

TRANSLATED FROM FRENCH BY PHYLLIS ARONOFF

THE AZRIELI FOUNDATION
www.azrielifoundation.org

Cover and book design by Mark Goldstein
Endpaper maps by Martin Gilbert
Maps on pages xxiv–xxv by François Blanc

LIBRARY AND ARCHIVES CANADA CATALOGUING IN PUBLICATION

Elias Quddus, Marguerite, 1936–
[Cachée. English] In hiding: a memoir illustrated by the author/ Marguerite Élias Quddus; translated from French by Phyllis Aronoff.

(Azrieli series of Holocaust survivor memoirs; 5)
Translation of: Cachée.
Includes bibliographical references and index.
ISBN 978-1-897470-36-7 (pbk.)

1. Elias Quddus, Marguerite, 1936–. 2. Holocaust, Jewish (1939–1945) – France – Personal narratives. 3. Jewish children in the Holocaust – France – Biography. 4. Holocaust survivors – Canada – Biography. I. Aronoff, Phyllis, 1945–, translator II. Azrieli Foundation III. Title. IV. Series: Azrieli series of Holocaust survivor memoirs. Series; V

D804.196.E5413 2013   940.53'18092   C2013-905033-7

The Azrieli Series of Holocaust Survivor Memoirs

Contents

Series Preface:
In their own words...

In telling these stories, the writers have liberated themselves. For so many years we did not speak about it, even when we became free people living in a free society. Now, when at last we are writing about what happened to us in this dark period of history, knowing that our stories will be read and live on, it is possible for us to feel truly free. These unique historical documents put a face on what was lost, and allow readers to grasp the enormity of what happened to six million Jews – one story at a time.

> *David J. Azrieli*, C.M., C.Q., M.Arch
> Holocaust survivor and founder, The Azrieli Foundation

Since the end of World War II, over 30,000 Jewish Holocaust survivors have immigrated to Canada. Who they are, where they came from, what they experienced and how they built new lives for themselves and their families are important parts of our Canadian heritage. The Azrieli Foundation's Holocaust Survivor Memoirs Program was established to preserve and share the memoirs written by those who survived the twentieth-century Nazi genocide of the Jews of Europe and later made their way to Canada. The program is guided by the conviction that each survivor of the Holocaust has a remarkable story to tell, and that such stories play an important role in education about tolerance and diversity.

Millions of individual stories are lost to us forever. By preserving the stories written by survivors and making them widely available to a broad audience, the Azrieli Foundation's Holocaust Survivor Memoirs Program seeks to sustain the memory of all those who perished at the hands of hatred, abetted by indifference and apathy. The personal accounts of those who survived against all odds are as different as the people who wrote them, but all demonstrate the courage, strength, wit and luck that it took to prevail and survive in such terrible adversity. The memoirs are also moving tributes to people – strangers and friends – who risked their lives to help others, and who, through acts of kindness and decency in the darkest of moments, frequently helped the persecuted maintain faith in humanity and courage to endure. These accounts offer inspiration to all, as does the survivors' desire to share their experiences so that new generations can learn from them.

The Holocaust Survivor Memoirs Program collects, archives and publishes these distinctive records and the print editions are available free of charge to libraries, educational institutions and Holocaust-education programs across Canada. They are also available for sale to the general public at bookstores.

The Azrieli Foundation would like to express appreciation to the following people for their invaluable efforts in producing this book: Sherry Dodson (Maracle Press), Sir Martin Gilbert, Farla Klaiman, Michael Quddus, and Margie Wolfe and Emma Rodgers of Second Story Press.

About the Glossary

The following memoir contains a number of terms, concepts and historical references that may be unfamiliar to the reader. For information on major organizations; significant historical events and people; geographical locations; religious and cultural terms; and foreign-language words and expressions that will help give context and background to the events described in the text, please see the glossary beginning on page 195.

Introduction

Out of the shadows and into the light…

Marguerite Élias Quddus tells us the story the history books do not tell: the turmoil of war as experienced by a very young child who has only a superficial understanding of the historical context. Little Marguerite takes us into her world before the war and her happy life within her family. The drawings and descriptions evoke a past world that is little known to most of us: the everyday life of an immigrant Jewish family in pre-World War II Paris. Although only a small child, Marguerite has already encountered antisemitism in the unkind comments the landlord has made to her father. But life is on the whole peaceful – until the war that plunges the lives of Marguerite and her family into terror.

The author has chosen to create a portrait of the little girl she was, with all her joys and sorrows, her ways of thinking and her values. Indeed, it is her hope that she will be read and understood by children, whose company she enjoys and to whom she relates very well.

But putting her memories into writing did not come easily to Marguerite. It took a particular event to precipitate the confrontation with her past. That event was the announcement of the impending demolition of 99 rue de Charonne, her childhood home before the war. She returned to that house before the work started and the flood of images that sprang into her mind brought her back to the dark years of the war. She wanted to write about them but was unable to do so. Her son, Michael, suggested that she draw her most painful memory. Using her artistic talent, she began with great difficulty to draw the scene of her parting with her father, when he was taken away in the first roundup in the 11th arrondissement, where the family lived. This initial drawing gave rise to an almost visceral need to create more drawings. It was not unusual for Marguerite to become so absorbed in her work, so oblivious to her surroundings, that she felt as if she were under a spell. Little by little, she reconstructed her past. After two years, the drawings were finished, with written explanations that, over time, would become an actual narrative.

Writing that narrative demanded such intensive work on her emotions that Marguerite says it was her therapy. Indeed, she did not merely enumerate the facts, she relived the feelings, which were often terrifying. She drew on her visual memory to enter into her past and on her musical sense to write: she put down the whole story in verse. She felt this music allowed the expression of her emotions to come more easily. However, in order to make the text lighter and more accessible to a broad public, it has been modified in our edition and returned to prose. But the main qualities of Marguerite's style have not been altered: the musicality of the writing, the succinctness of the sentences, the realistic quality of the dialogue, the immediacy of the present tense. The author has deliberately recreated the simple, even childish, language of the little girl she was, in order to give a voice to that child, who could not express herself. This means that the story can be read by young people as well as by adults without losing any of its richness and immediacy.

Both adults and children can understand the magical attraction the blue telephone has for Marguerite. A toy given to her after her father's arrest, it allows her to deal with the pain of his absence and, later, to endure the victimization of the family. The telephone is a marvellous symbol of freedom regained: the child can telephone whomever she wants, whenever and wherever she wants. It offers her the hope of being able to reach her world before the war merely through an imagined phone call – a hope that enables her to get through some very painful experiences.

In addition to the blue telephone, which gets left behind in Paris, there is another favourite toy that helps Marguerite and that goes with her into hiding: the doll given to her by her father on his return from the army at the Armistice. Both adults and children can recognize this doll as a symbol of the absent father. Little Marguerite is extremely attached to it and keeps it with her throughout the war. Marguerite has donated the doll to the Montreal Holocaust Memorial Centre, where it may be seen today.

The younger readers will recognize how authentic the arguments between Marguerite and her sister Henriette are: clearly, Marguerite refuses to soften reality to make it more "acceptable." However, it takes an adult's perspective to understand the psychosomatic nature of the symptoms Marguerite experiences each time her world turns upside down. When everything seems out of control, she too loses control and becomes incontinent. Thus the story is punctuated with references to diarrhea and bedwetting, revealing better than words the little girl's distress during the ordeal of her separation from her family.

~

The story told by Marguerite is both the personal experience of one little girl during the war and a page from collective history. The adults' actions and choices, as well as the French and international context, are seen through a child's eyes. Although they are not explored in detail by Marguerite, these larger actions and historical events frame her story and provide reference points for it.

When Germany defeated France in 1940 and an armistice was signed, France was split in two: the north was under German military occupation, while a southern zone, consisting of two-fifths of the country, was under the direct control of a new government established in the city of Vichy. Led by Marshal Pétain, a hero of World War I, the Vichy government collaborated with the Nazis. Pétain and his many supporters were not driven only by a desire to get France out of the war; they were also motivated by a wish for a "National Revolution" with a program to transform France into an authoritarian state that promoted traditional values, corporatism and xenophobia.

As in all the countries they occupied, the Germans quickly established anti-Jewish measures in the northern zone. At the same time, the Vichy government put in place its own measures against Jews and other "undesirables" – Communists, immigrants, Freemasons, Roma (called Gypsies at the time) and homosexuals, among others. Major decrees were passed; one in particular, the Statute on Jews, strictly defined the criteria for identifying a person as a Jew and assigned such persons a lower status in civil law for the admitted purpose of limiting their role in French society.

There were 350,000 Jews living in metropolitan France in 1940, the majority of whom were not of French nationality but had immigrated from eastern Europe after World War I or had fled Nazi Germany and other European countries in the 1930s. Of that number, 200,000 lived in Paris, among them Marguerite and her family. At the beginning of the occupation, the Jews of Paris and the northern zone lost the right to hold jobs and had their property confiscated. Many were arrested and subjected to restrictions on their movement and communication. As in the Vichy-governed free zone, the German anti-Jewish measures were initially aimed at non-nationals; thousands of people were arrested and interned in transit camps – among them Mr. Élias, the father of Henriette and Marguerite, despite his record of service in the French army.

In early 1942, the Vichy government and the Nazi occupiers began to work more closely with each other, and all Jews began to be targeted by discriminatory measures: the Jewish population of the occupied zone had to wear a yellow star to identify them, and their freedom of movement was taken away. The first *rafles* (roundups) of

Jews in the occupied zone started in 1941 and were carried out by the French police under German supervision. The best-known of the *rafles*, those of July 16 and 17, 1942, resulted in more than 12,000 Parisian Jews being taken to the Vélodrome d'Hiver, where they spent several days in crowded conditions before beginning the journey toward the Auschwitz death camp. At the same time, the Vichy government arrested many in the free zone. The deportations continued until the liberation of France in the summer of 1944. In all, 76,000 Jews from France were deported to the death camps in Germany and occupied Poland; only 2,500 of them came back alive.

While many of the French were angered by these measures, there was general apathy as long as the victims were mainly foreign nationals. The turning point in public opinion only came toward the end of 1942, when the roundups began to indiscriminately include refugees, immigrants and French nationals, men, women and children in both the northern zone and the southern zone.

Children as well as adults were targeted by the Nazis' genocidal policy. Between 1940 and 1944, there were 11,000 minors deported from France and murdered. Of these, 6,000 were under thirteen years old and 2,000 were under six years old.[1] It was in this context that Marguerite's mother decided in 1942 to hide her two little girls. She was helped by a network of clandestine organizations, both Jewish and non-Jewish, that had been set up to resist Nazi and Vichy oppression and save the largest possible number of persecuted children.

The organization that helped Marguerite's mother, the Service d'évacuation et de regroupement des enfants (SERE; Office of Evacuation and Regrouping of Children), was affiliated with the Œuvre de secours aux enfants (OSE; Children's Relief Agency). The OSE was a worldwide Jewish organization working in children's aid and public health. It set up a network in France that was known

---

1   Robert Rozett and Shmuel Spector, eds., *Encyclopedia of the Holocaust* (Jerusalem, 2000), 220–221, 352–353; Serge Klarsfeld, *Memorial to the Jews Deported From France, 1942–1944* (New York, 1983).

as the Garel circuit.[2] In September 1941, the OSE decided to hide Jewish children with non-Jewish families because its leadership had understood the terrifying implications of the discriminatory measures against them. So Marguerite and Henriette were placed among Catholics; several times, they were hidden in convents. Often, the members of OSE prepared the children by teaching them the basics of Catholicism. But at the same time, they tried as far as possible to give them an awareness of their family and religious background.[3] In Marguerite's story, it is the children's mother who introduces her daughters to Catholicism.

The mission of the OSE was to find families with whom Jewish children could be placed and to maintain contact once the children were with these families. They also had to fabricate false identification papers, obtain ration cards and pay the people hiding the children.[4] All this was done under very difficult conditions, where the overriding concern was the need for secrecy. Marguerite and Henriette went from one place to another – which was not unusual – and each time, they had escorts. Marguerite honours the memory of two of them, Estelle Eskenazi and Colette Mayer Wormser, dedicating her book to them. But the little girl she was during the war merely mentions these women without saying – how could she have known? – that they were risking their lives to bring the girls to the families. One situation in particular must have been especially dangerous: when the children went to meet their aunt Sonia, who lived in the southern zone, they had to cross the line of demarcation, which was under close surveillance. We can imagine the risks this entailed and admire the courage of the woman who escorted them.

There were many reasons why some civilians took the risk of

---

2   Yehuda Bauer, *American Jewry and the Holocaust: The American Joint Distribution Committee, 1939–1945* (Detroit: Wayne State University Press, 1981), 246–250.

3   Bauer, *American Jewry*, 249.

4   Ibid., 247.

hiding children in their homes. The incentive of extra income was not insignificant, but it alone does not explain such a decision. Serge Klarsfeld's statistics on children who were hidden show that France was one of the German-occupied countries of Europe in which the highest number of Jewish children were saved.[5]

~

Marguerite's story gives us a glimpse of the experience of a great many children in France and Europe during this period. Saved from certain death, these children nonetheless bore the scars of the trauma they endured during the war. They often had to confront fundamental questions of identity after the war. In many cases, non-Jewish aid organizations and Catholic families tried to convert the children in their charge. Even when this did not happen, the children naturally felt affection for the adults who protected them, and some felt torn at the end of the war, even when they were lucky enough to reunite with their families – of whom they sometimes had only a distant memory. Both adults and children can readily grasp the terrible dilemma Marguerite faced when she had to decide whether to call the people hiding her and taking care of her for a year Papa and Mama. The child had the impression that in giving these names to her adoptive parents, she was erasing the memory of her real parents, whom she constantly thought about, especially her father, to whom she was particularly attached. During the three years of separation, Marguerite remained absolutely faithful to them.

Marguerite's story is also interesting in that it reveals a whole range of attitudes toward Jews. There are antisemites, collaborators and informers, but there is also a friend of the Élias family who supports and protects them by every means in her power. A few people show goodwill despite the fact that Jews are pariahs. Among the allies

---

5   Klarsfeld, *Memorial to the Jews*.

are a farming couple, the Chatenays, who welcome the little girls and greatly contribute to their survival. There are also all the people who help but expect payment, or those who get cold feet when the risk becomes too great. Finally, we must not forget the mass of people who are totally indifferent to the situation of Jews and do not help them in any way.

For Marguerite and for all the children who were hidden, bearing witness by writing about their clandestine life is important both individually and collectively. Individually, because in order to deal with the painful reality of those years of separation and fear, they must be able to talk about them. Marguerite never had the opportunity of sharing with her family, particularly her mother, the story of her life in hiding. The watchword in her immediate environment seems to have been that what happened in the past stayed in the past, and it was important to look to the future. But those years did not remain quiet and painless in a corner of her memory; they constantly intruded into the present. The desire to bear witness became a necessity. Moreover, the wish to transmit this part of her personal history to her son, Michael, was also a very strong motivation.

Collectively, it is important to bear witness because future generations have a duty to learn the lessons of the war – the why and the how, but also the moral value of those who were involved in it, both as military personnel and as civilians. We must pay homage to the women and men who had the courage to take risks in order to help their neighbours and denounce those who chose to inform on them and collaborate with their oppressors.

The story of the children who were hidden has become a subject of current interest and research. Now, at the beginning of the twenty-first century, the youngest survivors of the Holocaust are, increasingly, the only ones who can still bear direct witness. Because of the clandestine nature of the rescue operations – the identities of the children had to be protected above all – existing official documents on the hidden children are often in code and are not very informative.

Direct accounts are therefore an essential source for understanding this aspect of the war and Marguerite's story thus has a place in collective history.

Two other things make this document extraordinary: the material on the post-war period and the use of illustrations. Marguerite does not end her story with the liberation; she continues it beyond. Indeed, for her, the child in hiding, the separation from her family was not over after the end of the war. Her life could never go on "as before" because the war had obliterated that "before."

The fact that this story is illustrated by the author herself makes it particularly valuable. The drawings, with their freshness and candour, allow us to enter immediately into the world of the child. They not only enhance the story, they also provide additional detail on everyday life such as the parents' workshop, the home on rue de Charonne, the clothing, the doctor and his cupping glasses and the scenes of farm life.

As the Israeli writer Aharon Appelfeld points out, "Only art has the power to transform suffering and deliver us from the abyss."[6] Marguerite's whole project involves this transformation through expression; it enables the adult woman to bring the child she once was out of the shadows and into the light.

Elizabeth Lasserre and Naomi Azrieli
August 2007
Toronto

---

6 Aharon Appelfeld, *Beyond Despair* (New York: Fromm International, 1993).

SOURCES

Marrot-Fellag Ariouet, Céline. "Les Enfants cachés pendant la Seconde Guerre mondiale aux sources de l'histoire clandestine." In *La Maison des enfants de Sèvres*, <http://lamaisondesevres.org/cel/celsom.html>. Consulted March 15, 2012.

Bauer, Yehuda. *American Jewry and the Holocaust: The American Joint Distribution Committee, 1939–1945*. Detroit: Wayne State University Press, 1981.

Jackson, Julian. *France: The Dark Years, 1940–1944*. Oxford: Oxford University Press, 2003.

Krell, Robert. "Child Survivors of the Holocaust: The Elderly Children and Their Adult Lives." In *And Life is Changed Forever: Holocaust Childhoods Remembered*. Edited by Martin Ira Glassner and Robert Krell. Detroit: Wayne State University Press, 2006.

Marks, Jane. *Hidden Children: The Secret Survivors of the Holocaust*. New York: Ballantine Books, 1993.

Marrus, Michael R., and Robert O. Paxton. *Vichy France and the Jews*. New York: Basic Books, 1981.

Paxton, Robert O. *Vichy France*. New York: Knopf, 1972.

Rousso, Henry. *The Vichy Syndrome: History and Memory in France Since 1944*. Translated by Arthur Goldhammer. Cambridge: Harvard University Press, 1991.

Rozett, Robert, and Shmuel Spector, eds. *Encyclopedia of the Holocaust*. Jerusalem: Yad Vashem/Jerusalem Publishing House, 2000.

Maps

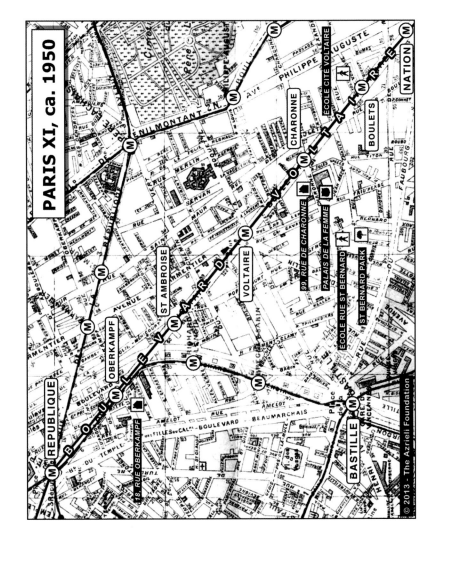

PARIS XI, ca. 1950

This book is dedicated
To the memory of my beloved father, Maurice Élias (Srol Moïse Éliash), a voluntary recruit to the military, demobilized at the Armistice, who was taken from our house on August 20, 1941, and interned in the Drancy camp until December 12, 1941. On that day, he was transferred to the Compiègne camp from which he was deported to Auschwitz on March 27, 1942. On April 19, 1942, at the age of thirty-six, after eight months of privation and humiliation, he was murdered.

To my mother, Rachel Perl Élias (née Sandler), whose courage, strength and determination saved us in spite of ourselves. In 1944, she took part in the operations of the French Forces of the Interior (FFI) for the Union des juifs pour la résistance et l'entraide (UJRE; Union of Jews for Assistance and Resistance), in the Lyon combat group. She survived until 1996.

To Estelle Eskenazi and Colette Mayer Wormser, assistants in the social services of Notre-Dame-de-Sion in Grenoble, who escorted us at the risk of their lives. They were known under the names Estelle Évrard and Colette Morel in the Service d'évacuation et de regroupement des enfants (SERE; Office of Evacuation and Regrouping of Children), which was associated with the Œuvre de secours aux enfants (OSE; Children's Relief Agency).

To Madame Graziani, a faithful and brave friend to my parents.

To my aunt Sonia Zanditénas and all those who helped me during those dangerous times.

To my paternal grandfather, Icek Éliash, his son Abraham and his grandson Bobi, who were killed as hostages in Lithuania. To my grandmother Méra Tow Éliash, Icek's wife, and my maternal grandmother, Gindé Dvaure Sandler (née Mayer), and her daughter, my aunt Sarah, all of whom were massacred. Not to mention the other members of my family – uncles, aunts and cousins – who died in the prime of life.

To Raphaël Sandler, Mama's younger brother, who died in Stalingrad fighting for freedom.

And to Nicolas Quddus, my grandson, born on November 17, 2011.

Acknowledgements

To my husband, Dr. Abdul Quddus, whose moral and material support enabled me to devote seven years to this work, often at his expense.

To my son, Michael Élias Quddus, who gave me his time, his resources, his love, and enough patience to handle the publication of the first edition of this book himself.

To my sister, Ariette Élias Massardo, who died on May 6, 2007, in overwhelming distress due to her painful past. She was my sole companion during a childhood marked by the destruction of our family. We lived together in shame over our origins, which we had to cover up for fear of horrific consequences, until we were finally reunited with our mother.

To all my friends near and far who had faith in me and encouraged me.

To Daniel Gorfinkel (Israel), René Goldman (Vancouver, Canada) and Bernard Ebenstein of Limoges (France), brothers in misery when we lived together in the home for the children of deportees in Andrésy, in 1945.

To Mr. and Mrs. Robert Chatenay, in France, who sheltered me for eighteen months in extraordinary, frightening conditions. The meetings I had with them after the war (some held in secret to spare my mother's feelings) and the oftentimes emotional correspondence we kept after I was married, helped us realize how important our relationship was in my life and that of my new family.

Today, both my family and I still have a strong relationship with the Chatenays' nephew, Mr. Michel, and his family in Cras (Isère region).

To Bernard Hanau, who remained in hiding at the Chatenays' farm for ten months. He was unaware that my sister and I were Jewish and vice versa. I found him after the war but he was lost again too soon; and to Claudine, his widow, who kept up our special connection after his death.

Author's Preface

I was born when times were good, on December 4, 1936, in Paris, in the 19th arrondissement. My parents were living comfortably from their business in the most working-class neighbourhood of the city, with the help of a workman and a maid. My sister was two years old. Our apartment was located near boulevard Voltaire, in the middle of rue de Charonne, upstairs from our neighbour's bistro and our store and workshop. It was situated right in the heart of the "revolutionary triangle" formed by the Place de la Bastille, the Place de la République and the Place de la Nation.

My father, the grandson of the great kabbalist Éliashev, had had to flee his native Russia with his whole family at the age of ten because of the pogroms. A refugee in Lithuania, he met the woman who was to become his wife in June 1931 in Paris, in the 14th arrondissement. In 1925, he had chosen to settle in democratic France and study law, which his brother Abraham was already practising in Lithuania. He attended university for two years while working as a porter at the Gare de Lyon in order to be financially independent of his parents. At the same time, he learned the furrier trade, at which he rapidly became a master.

On March 8, 1933, after working for other people and then in their own workshop, my parents opened a store at 99 rue de

Charonne. On January 30, 1935, my sister was born in Paris, in the 12th arrondissement.

On September 11, 1939, Papa applied to become a voluntary military recruit. On March 21, 1940, having been accepted, he joined the 212th Infantry Regiment, and on August 13, 1940, he was demobilized.

On September 27, 1940, a German ordinance forced Jews to register at police stations and government administrations. My father, respectful of the law, complied. Later, the rounding up of Jews would be made easier by this census.

On October 18, 1940, administrators were appointed to Jewish businesses. Ours was named Léonce Tourne. A copy of one of his threatening letters is included in the appendix.

On October 19, 1940, Jews in the occupied zone had their identity cards stamped with the word *JUIF*.

On April 26, 1941, Jews in the occupied zone were barred from a number of professional activities. The administrators appointed to Jewish businesses were given the right to sell them to Aryans or liquidate them.

On May 14, 1941, the first *rafle* (roundup) of Jews took place in Paris.

On August 13, 1941, the order was given to confiscate radios and bicycles belonging to Jews. I clearly remember losing our phones at the same time even though the official removal of phones from all Jewish homes by the Postes, Télégraphes et Téléphones, the government communications monopoly, was carried out on June 2, 1941.

On August 20, 1941, a massive roundup of Jews took place in the 11th arrondissement. It was the first one to target the Jewish population in that specific part of Paris. Papa was arrested at home, at dawn, by three Frenchmen, and taken to the Drancy camp.

On December 12, 1941, one thousand Jewish intellectuals and influential people, most of them French nationals, were arrested in Paris. The same day, the police handed Papa over to the occupation authorities.

On February 7, 1941, a German order was issued that severely curtailed freedom of movement and imposed a curfew on Jews between 8 p.m. and 6 a.m. Furthermore, Jews were no longer allowed to change their place of residence.

On March 27, 1942, the first deportation of French Jews was carried out; one thousand prominent Jews were sent to the death camps. Papa was part of the first convoy.

On April 19, 1942, my father was murdered at the Auschwitz death camp.

On May 29, 1942, Jews aged six and over in the occupied zone were ordered to wear a yellow star "solidly sewn onto their clothing."

On July 8, 1942, Jews were forbidden to go to theatres, restaurants, parks, etc. They were allowed to shop only between 3 p.m. and 4 p.m.

Out of the 76,000 Jews deported from France, only 2,500 came back.

~

The beginning of my story takes place in 1941 and is followed by a brief look back at my family's flight from Paris in 1940, during what is known as the *Exode*. I reconstruct the historical image of 99 rue de Charonne. I recall the atmosphere of my childhood years that had happiness and joy followed by distress and suffering. I remember my fear and my rebellion against injustice and lack of understanding. I tell of the series of adaptations my sister and I were forced to make, how we had no choice but to accept our guardians, and how this resulted in feelings of guilt.

I had to bury the happy period of my early years when I was spoiled along with the unhappy war years. I felt pressure to avoid any mention of these difficult times. I should have been listened to in order to be able to face the problems haunting me and deal with the new ones that arose. But I was categorically forbidden to speak of my experience and I could not think about it without feeling guilty. My judgment didn't count; my suffering didn't exist. After the war, I was held back two years at school. At eleven, I earned the first prize in my class but, because I was older than the other children, their parents put pressure on the administration of the school to take my prize away. The Cité Voltaire school yielded to them. Furthermore, I needed a special dispensation to be allowed to enrol in high school, but it was mercilessly refused.

I show what the burden of secrecy did to us. My sister, weighed down by too many responsibilities, was unable to exercise her authority over me without being tempted to abuse it.

I express my recognition and gratitude to everyone who helped and protected me in spite of the determination of our country to rob our parents and allow the Germans to murder us.

I denounce the Vichy administrators to whom we had to turn over our property and who forced us to hide like criminals in order to save our lives at all costs.

I have written this book in order to immortalize the tragedy that marked our lives and to commemorate my parents, who were loved and respected by so many. I also wished to honour my father's life so that his brief existence was not in vain. In telling this story, I was able to truly process the nightmare I had lived through during the most difficult part of my childhood and express my unresolved pain. Finally, I needed to free myself from the residual guilt and shame I had felt for too long about my Jewish identity.

Part One:

UNDER MY PARENTS' PROTECTION

The street of my love, the street where I came into the world.

Happiness

Nestled in my fortress of pillows, I'm resting to re-
cover from my cold. A warm caress tickles the
end of my nose and multicoloured spots dance
in front of my closed eyes. I sleep and sleep and
sleep and sleep... because if I want to go outside,
I have to get better.

The radio is playing "The street of our love...
You see them there at night, the lovers in dark corners...." It's a song my parents love and it makes them
waltz.

The whir of Mama's sewing machine has started up again faster
than ever, *rrr... rrr... rrr... rrr...* again and again. They've put me in an
armchair facing the open window; my sheets are fluttering like the
leaves of a tree in the wind. The motion of the sewing machine makes
the legs of the chair vibrate. It feels like the rumbling of a train engine
and it takes me to the land of dreams. I dream a thou-
sand stories and I forget what's around me.

I let the sound of the train lull me. The cars keep
on going by. STOP! Everybody off! The shaking
has stopped and so has the noise. Only the music
continues on its melodious way. I don't want to
close my eyes and I call, "Mama! Mama!" Nobody
hears me. My mother at her sewing machine
coughs slightly, takes a puff of her cigarette, takes
another piece of fabric to overcast and starts again,

even faster. Her smoke goes up to the sky and I float up astride it without leaving my street.

The telephone rings. One, two, three rings. I mustn't pick up before the fourth ring. I wanted to take this call but someone already has. I'm not lucky today.

When Auntie Sonia talks to me, it lasts a long time, so long that sometimes our conversation gets cut off. But she calls me right back to say, "See you soon!" Sonia is so pretty, with her golden hair and sky-blue eyes. She wears such nice perfume that I give her lots of hugs and kisses so it will rub off on me and I'll smell like her. She spoils us when she comes. Everyone loves her.

The sunlight makes me blink and I'm not cold anymore. I greet it with joy! I open the neck of my nightgown and bask in the warmth. A feeling of well-being envelops me. I have to get better.

This morning, Papa said we would all go to the country next summer. He found a house with a garden all around it. We'll be able to run through the grass there, barefoot of course, and shout all we want without anyone scolding us. I can't wait to go there and play with him every day.

My Dog Choukette

On the table, there's a plate filled with cookies, squares of chocolate and a cube of sugar for Choukette. And a glass of milk for me. I drink it in one gulp.

Curled up beside the bed, her muzzle in the air, quivering with longing, Choukette is waiting for the signal that she can share the feast. We're going to have a party. Her ears prick up and she's ready to jump up. "Come on, girl!" I say. She stands up on her hind legs and begs, barking, but I make her suffer. Without getting out from under my blankets, I pick up the precious white cube that draws her like a magnet. While she dances with excitement, I pitilessly hold her reward out of her reach. In one bound, she leaps up higher than usual – so high that she loses her balance – and grabs the sugar in her mouth. She crunches it loudly, wagging her tail the way only she can, and I tease her, saying, "It's good, isn't it. You like that, don't you?"

She gives me a pleading look, as if to say, "Why don't you let me into your warm nest?" Then, of course, I hold out my arms to her and there she is beside me, licking my face with her sticky tongue. But what do I care, as long as she doesn't bite me! She's never mean to me. I wipe my face on my sleeve. I stroke her back from her neck to her tail. "Do, re, mi, fa, so, la, ti, do." You must never stroke an animal's coat the wrong way, that's what Mama says.

Choukette has curly hair like a lamb. She's all white except for a black spot on the front of her neck that distinguishes her from other poodles. But you don't have to go looking for her, she never gets lost. She has such a good nose that she could smell me from the ends of the earth. When we're outside, I don't have to call her a lot and possibly bother people in the neighbourhood. She knows where she mustn't go.

We've eaten all the treats, and I'm full. I lie down quietly again with the taste of chocolate in my mouth. We're so nice and warm, the two of us. She lolls on the soft down quilt, a gift from Mama's mother, like the pillows – one for each granddaughter, but right now, all mine.

Unfortunately, I don't know my grandmothers or my grandfathers. They're too far away. When my parents talk about them, I have to keep quiet because it makes them sad. My sister is coming home from school. Let's not make a sound.

Madame Hortense's Bistro

"Whoa! Whoa now!" calls the wine merchant, stopping his horses in front of our neighbour's bistro. Madame Hortense opens the trap

door to the basement for the delivery men, and, one after the other, they carry the cases of wine down in their arms or on their backs and pile them up neatly. Then they climb back up. The owner closes the trap door, calling, "Come have a glass at the bar, fellows. It's on me!" The spigots are open all day. Meanwhile, the manure drops into the gutter. That smell will stay with me. It reminds me of the *Exode*, the flight from Paris, because it's the same smell as in the stable where we took refuge.

Papa enlists as a volunteer, 1939–1940.

The Exode *from Paris*

I hate the Germans because of the bombing. We had to get out as fast as possible to get away from it. "Thank goodness we didn't give away the stroller," Mama kept saying, very upset. "This could keep up for a long time!" We get the stroller out of the workshop and put some basic necessities in it. Then we lock the door, leaving Choukette barking frantically. Unfortunately, she has to stay and guard the house.

We weave our way through the people, some of whom I know. "Hurry up, Marguerite!" I never go fast enough, so Mama has me climb into the stroller, but she takes me out when we go downhill and when we go uphill. It's too heavy; it takes two men to lift it and they're not easy to find when everyone is in a rush. But when Mama of-fers them money, two men agree to help us. First, the métro. Even in first class, it's uncomfortable. There's not enough room. Then we take a train, which is also packed this morning. At the sta-tion, everyone is talking about the war. Mama makes me get on first. Someone is blocking the entrance and we're stuck at the end of the car. With some difficulty, Mama manages to get my sister and me seated on top of our things. A fat woman, who doesn't smell nice, is between us and our mother. If Papa were here, he would have found us a better place, but he's in the army.

In the Army!

My Papa was so handsome in his soldier's uniform, with his cap and his gold buttons. Ever since I vis-ited him in the army, I've been wanting to cry. We went to the barracks, all three of us, at least twice. Mama is always telling the story.

We visited his dormitory, which was so smoky you could be asphyxiated! Except for Papa, almost all the soldiers go around with cigarettes in their mouths. He slipped his cartons of cigarettes to "Rachel" – that was what he called her there, or else, "honey."

My sister called out the names of all the things she saw, from the chairs to the beds. She likes attention. I didn't dare try to stop her. I kept quiet to please Papa. He doesn't like us to show off.

We were wearing our pink Sunday dresses and white socks, with patent leather shoes and purses. He was happy to see us. He hugged me and put away the cologne we had brought him in his trunk. "Your dolls are lovely and their clothes are beautiful!" said one of his buddies to tease him. And he answered proudly, "You should tell that to my wife – she's the one who dressed them!"

His new friends seemed nice, but they weren't very polite. My father didn't let them say bad words in front of us, especially not "you bastard." Their language didn't bother me at all – I thought it was funny. It was more fun than hearing them talk about the old days. They made toasts – "To health!" and "To peace!" and "To going back home!" – knocking back the cognac we'd brought. We shared the cheesecake (my favourite) that Mama had baked in her Jewish cake tin. They loved it.

Then it was time for goodbyes. Papa and Mama shared one last private conversation that was followed by a sad silence because we were parting. Then Papa said, "I'll see you soon, my dear little girls. Be good to your mother!" My parents held each other for a very long time in the corner of the vestibule. The hands of the clock said it was time to leave. We hugged very hard and left without looking back.

The Farm in Fontainebleau

It was already dark when we got there, but the farmer's wife hadn't left a light on. "You've come too late. I'm full up. Do you understand French? I have no more room," she said in a low voice.

"Put us wherever you can. We're so tired," Mama insisted, taking out another wad of bills. "Look, here's an advance. The place doesn't matter."

"My dear Madame Élias, I'm sorry. All I have left is the stable, on the straw."

Where does she want us to go? In the stable? Is that really what she said? They're walking while they talk and Henriette is running ahead of them. We have to cross the farmyard among the chickens, ducks and geese. Amid the cacophony of quacking, even the rabbits have something to say. The pigs are very frightening. One of them sniffs at my legs with a wet snout. I'm petrified.

"Hurry, dear!" cries Mama. I slowly go forward. The cows' eyes shine as I come near them. They look ferocious. The horses are tied up at the gate. Instead of cattle, there are whole families lying in rows on the ground. With the help of Henriette, Mama drags the stroller to a dark corner.

They spread out a blanket and put the pillows on it. And, wearing my fur coat, I lie down beside Mama, who's also wearing hers. I complain, "It's itchy!"

"Stop that whining. Go to sleep and don't make a fuss," she scolds.

Obediently, I curl up in my nest.

I wake up suddenly to the sound of a baby crying until its mother gives it her breast. I hear the rumble of bombing in the distance. I'm cold. I'm shivering all over. I have to pee. I nudge Mama, softly at first, and then harder and harder. Her mouth is open and she's snoring.

My sister has thrown her covers off and, worse, she's delirious. I squeeze my buttocks together, wriggling. I shout into the silence, "Mama, hurry! Mama! Mama!" But it's too late, it's coming.

"Can't you see you're disturbing your sister? She has a fever."

I bite my lips in shame. "I went in my pants."

"What are you saying?"

"I went in my pants!"

She pulls my clothes up and dries me roughly, angrily. After throwing the soiled clothes on the manure pile, she turns off the flashlight. I curl up again without a peep and fall asleep.

The next morning at the rooster's crow, all the Parisians are manoeuvring to be first to go and wash. Henriette has vomited again. I take advantage of the situation to run off and see what's going on outside. I barely miss stepping in a cow pie, how horrible!

In the afternoon, my sister is better. Instead of eating like everyone else, she starts telling stories again, but nobody scolds her. I drink as much milk as I can before we leave for home. We have no more money, but lots of parcels: fresh eggs, butter, ham and the farmers' famous dry sausage.

We find Choukette, who's sick because she hasn't had her walks. I hold her in my arms. It's so good to be home!

Armistice

It took some time before Papa left his regiment and came back home. "Luckily, it's the slow season," Mama kept saying. Choukette was the first to recognize him, from the end of the street. He was walking in a dignified way, like a soldier. Even the police saluted him as he passed, in front of all the neighbours. It was the end of summer. He was giving candies to the kids in the neighbourhood.

Then he put down his bag and sat down in front of the shop and took me in his lap. Touching his face, I cried, "It's all prickly!" And he answered, laughing, "It's not as soft as fur, but it's better!" We celebrated until midnight and then we went to bed.

My Sister's Violin

Today Henriette has her violin lesson. You don't hear anything but her in the house. She has no school on Thursday, the day Mademoiselle Aubertin comes from morning until noon. Each lesson starts with scales and then goes on to a piece. Today she's practising "Twinkle, twinkle little star." That instrument is merciless! There's nothing that tortures my ears the way it does! All I can do is cover them.

The conscientious pupil practises without stopping in order to be praised: "You've really made progress! That was perfect! You're becoming an excellent violinist!" Why didn't she choose the piano?

When Hélène plays the piano upstairs, it doesn't bother me at all. On the contrary, I'd like to be able to play like her.

Mademoiselle Aubertin keeps smiling at me and I know what that means. With each smile, she's asking if I want to learn the violin. Nobody understands the effect that instrument has on me! When the bow strokes the strings, it sets my teeth on edge. The violin is too big and heavy, and my arms are too short. No, it's not for me. I'd rather draw pictures, like the artists who work around the Basilica of the Sacré-Cœur. So I keep refusing Mademoiselle Aubertin.

Tired of listening to them, I go to my room, under my bed, with my friends, Choukette and my dolls. But wouldn't you know it, Mademoiselle Aubertin – I recognize her feet – sits down right above me. She plays "The Blue Danube" and I feel like waltzing, but I can't move. I hug Choukette and she wags her tail against my face. Mademoiselle Aubertin whispers sweetly, "Don't you want to try it? Really?" I'm not as stupid as she thinks. I hesitate before answering, "No."

"Don't you like music?"

"Yes, but the piano is nicer!"

"And don't you like me? I hardly ever see you anymore. Your father would be so proud if you played the violin too."

"I already told you. No."

"And don't you like chocolates? Look, I've kept a few for you."

She lowers her hand, which is filled with sweet-smelling morsels, and holds it right near my nose! They're so tempting that I have a hard time restraining Choukette, who's whimpering. She leans over the side of the bed. "Goodbye, sweetie! I'll see you soon, I hope. I'll

have to give them to your sister. She'll enjoy them."

I wait until she goes back to Henriette and run to the kitchen with Choukette to drink the glass of milk that's waiting for me. The dog has her nose in the air. She has a great sense of smell, the little rascal! She smelled the chocolates on the table. That's amazing! There they are in the bowl, just for us. I break them into pieces, keeping the biggest one for me. "Come on, sit up and beg!" And she jumps up and snatches the chocolate.

Georgette Makes the Difference

Henriette has Mama's brown hair, but hers is as straight as sticks! That's why she pulls mine, she wants to make it uncurl. Just because she's two years older, it doesn't mean I have to follow her like a goose! I'm chubby because I take after Mama, but I look like Papa. Henriette says that isn't so, but I don't listen to her.

Henriette is so very picky during meals that Georgette, our maid, is always lecturing her. "You're going to get sick if you don't eat more. At your age, you have to eat. Your mother is right when she says you're as thin as a rake. Good lord! And she buys all these good things for you."

The skinny girl makes a grimace of disgust. It doesn't bother her at all. I enjoy drinking milk. She persists in hating it. I savour my soft-boiled egg with buttered bread. She says she can't bring herself to swallow eggs unless they're in an omelette or hard-boiled. She won't even taste mashed potatoes! She only likes crisp French fries.

Georgette fulfills my desires

and I eat everything she gives me, down to the last crumb. It's funny when she tells Mama, "I swear, if the older one doesn't eat anything, it's because you give in to her every wish!" Henriette has no problem with dessert – she likes them all. She'll even stick her spoon into my pudding and eat it! But I'll gladly give her my share of pineapple. She loves that and gobbles it right up.

Georgette treats us to pâtés, apple pies and, because she comes from Brittany, delicious and thick buckwheat pancakes. She takes food very seriously. My parents say she is "custom made" for us, the way they custom make the fur coats for their clients.

We Eat in the Kitchen

When we're alone at home we eat in the kitchen, but if there are guests we eat in the dining room, which looks out onto the corner of the courtyard. It's so close to our neighbour Madame Hortense's window that I could stand on a chair and shake her hand to say "Hello" with-

out losing my balance. We some-times get change from her to go to the store, reaching out to take it with the tips of our fingers, but I'd rather go to her bistro and drink a glass of milk or a deli-cious *diabolo* (mint syrup mixed with water) or, if it's cold out, a hot chocolate. There are always a  lot of men there – even some Germans! They're not mean. They call her by her first name and they give me candy.

At mealtimes, I sit in my straw booster seat set up on top of the couch because I'm so small. My sister would like to have a straw booster seat too, but she has to make do with the telephone book under her. She thinks she's smarter than I am because she's first in her class and can read the newspaper. Papa says that's normal, because she's learned to read. I console myself with the thought that it will soon be my turn. I hope my schoolbag won't be as heavy as hers.

From up on my chair, I deliberately let the pieces of fat that I don't like fall to the floor for Choukette, who loves them and begs for more.

Henriette has hardly started eating when I've finished my plate. "You should be ashamed!" Mama lectures her, upset that she doesn't like the delicious dinner that has been prepared. Then my parents say something that really hurts: "You should follow Marguerite's example!" Henriette gives me a dirty look, making it clear that she'll get back at me. But as long as they're watching her, I don't need to worry.

When Papa gets angry and frowns, it's a warning to us that we have to behave. When he puts his index finger to his mouth, you could hear a pin drop. Otherwise, you'll get a spanking. You were warned. But I've never actually been spanked.

My parents eat at the corner of the table, sharing one plate between them like lovers, but they each have their own cutlery. And they share one glass, too, supposedly because it makes fewer dishes to wash. The truth is that it gives them the opportunity to whisper mysterious things to each other in their foreign language.

We're supposed to eat in silence. I'm never the one who starts to talk because, first of all, "Good children don't chatter while they're eating," and second, "It's rude to talk with your mouth full," and third, "It's not polite to interrupt adults." Watch out! We're punished if we don't obey. Our parents are strict.

Photograph of my first birthday party. There were a lot of guests who are not shown here.

The Blue Shop

We live upstairs from our shop and workshop and the café. In the vestibule, there's a stairway that goes up to our apartment on the next floor. On the sign suspended between our two front windows, it says in white letters on a blue background À L'ARTISAN FOURREUR (The

Artisan Furrier). You can't miss it. And there's a fox in the centre. You can see it from far away.

Our shop window is blue, and so are the walls and the drapes inside. It goes well with the furs. The shop sells coats, jackets, linings, fur trim and so on. There are displays of hats, mittens and slippers in sheepskin and Persian lamb. There are even insoles of all sizes to put in shoes.

My parents are artisans. They make clothes from the tanned skins of animals that they buy from dealers. They know how to choose the skins, match them, cut them, wet them and tack them down with a hammer. Using special pliers, they stretch them in all directions and let them dry on a board. Using chalk, they trace around cardboard patterns. And then they cut off the extra fur, which automatically removes the marks. Finally, they join the pieces to each other and sew them together on the machine.

It's fascinating. I watch them work until the end of their workday when they roll down the metal shutter. The next morning, they adjust the pieces on the mannequin or on the client. They also restyle old models into beautiful new ones. Our customers say they're magicians and my parents enjoy the compliment.

When my sister leaves for school, I go behind the door of the shop and put my nose up against the glass, waiting impatiently for someone to come in. But as soon as a customer arrives, I go away. I go to the back, to the workshop, and watch through the lace of the curtain, standing still with my hands clasped behind my back. It's fun watching from my hiding place! The women chat with Mama and they strut around in front of the three-way mirror, striking all kinds of poses. I quietly imitate them. I can stay there like that all day if I want. It's like at the puppet show, but I laugh silently. While they're trying things on, I'm very good. "Another day over! We've earned it," say my parents with a sigh, tired but happy.

In winter, the whole family wears fur, even Papa. He has a grey

"There was fur everywhere, even on the beds." Photograph from my first birthday, December 4, 1936.

Indian lamb collar on his coat and a matching hat. Mama has more fur trim than he does.

I have two outfits in rabbit's fur. The first one, in wild rabbit and white, is for Sundays. It consists of a coat, a pillbox hat with ribbon ties and, to keep my hands warm, a muff hanging from my neck by a cord. I really like it. The second one, in brown castorette with a hood and mittens, is for weekdays. It doesn't get dirty as easily. I also have a whole ferret with paws, head and tail. Mama stuffed it. She put a form in its muzzle, gave it glass eyes that shine from every angle and put stuffing in its body. Before I put it around my neck, I shake it very hard and make it move like a puppet. The girls stroke it gently and the boys are all afraid of it.

Sundays with the Family

We sleep in. At sunrise, we tiptoe to our parents' room and slip into their bed. We take turns being in the middle. We never argue or we'd be sent back to our own beds. Papa puts his arm under my neck and I fall asleep against him. When the alarm clock goes off at ten o'clock, he gets up right away and without saying a word goes to take his shower at the municipal baths.

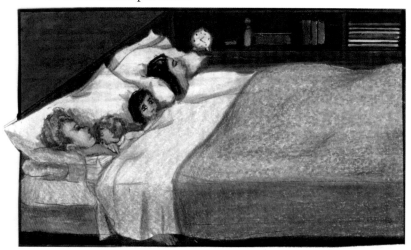

When he comes back, Mama leaves. She stays longer than he does, washing herself in a bath-tub and then spending hours at the hairdresser. She's so beautiful when she comes back that Papa calls her "my love." While we're waiting for her, Papa fills the tub in the kitchen half-full of hot water and puts us in. He soaps our backs and then pours water from a basin over our heads. I protect my eyes with my bath mitt. We laugh and splash water everywhere. Afterward, he rubs us dry with a towel and we get dressed while he wipes up the water on the floor. We feel like climbing on his back but it's not the right time for that – everything has to be clean when Mama gets home.

We quickly eat leftovers from yesterday's supper and plan our afternoon, depending on the weather. If it's sunny, we go to the Jardin du Luxembourg, our favourite place. If the weather is not as good, the Tuileries, the Bois de Boulogne or the Bois de Vincennes, which is nearest to our house. If it's raining, we go to Uncle Léon's or, more often, Auntie Sonia's, at the Strasbourg-St-Denis métro stop. She lives at 67 rue Notre-Dame-de-Nazareth.

We go to the movies, too. Henriette has to finish everything on her plate to deserve it. I prefer the puppet show, with Guignol, who tells stories and asks us questions. He tells us his secrets and shares with us how concerned he is about the bad guys, but he catches them every time! He hits them with his club and there's a happy ending. We scream so loudly, you can hear us for miles. Our parents wait quietly, sitting on the bench. Papa reads, Mama knits and they talk to each other. Today, because the weather is good, we've decided to go to the Luxembourg Gardens. We're taking the métro.

We get on at Charonne and

say hello to a few people we know. We get off across the street from the huge garden. We ride on the merry-go-round and Papa rents two little sailboats for us that sail away on the water. I run around the big pond, keeping my eyes glued to my boat. When it comes near the side, I push it back with a stick. My parents watch us.

They buy us a wooden hoop that's almost as tall as I am. I roll it along in front of me, tapping it with a little stick – a tap on the side to make it stand up and a tap on the edge to make it go faster. I fall and get dirty, which makes Mama unhappy although she comforts me anyway. "It's all right, dear." But if I hurt myself, it's all over. Then I have to sit beside her and amuse myself by counting birds or ladies in their hats.

When we take the bicycle, we put it in Nicolas' taxi. Nicolas is a friend of Papa's who lives at 97 rue de Charonne. He makes us laugh all the way and we never get bored. Papa put a wooden handle behind the saddle and I hold on to it, sitting behind Henriette because it's her bicycle. There's a bar that extends out on each side of the wheels that I can even stand up on. What I don't like is when she tells stories; when we fall, she always blames me. But it's not my fault if she loses control. "Sit straight, Marguerite!" Luckily, my father runs fast, and he's always close behind us.

When we go back to Mama, the picnic is ready. If it's really nice out, we go for a drink at the bar afterward and stay until evening. We go home in the dark, tired but happy.

Choukette Pees on the Landlord's Wall

"Papa! Papa! Choukette peed on Monsieur Gellé's wall! He hit her and she ran away!" The rude man is yelling with rage and disgust. "Dirty Jew's dog! Pisses all over the place!"

"No, not all over!" Papa says and proudly adds in a serious voice, "Dirty Jews' dogs know where to piss, Monsieur!"

Holidays in the Slow Season

On holidays in the slow season, my parents work in the workshop while we play in the courtyard. We have the courtyard to ourselves since the electromechanic plant that occupies part of our building is closed. We run and shout at the top of our lungs with the concierge's

children, who live seven in one room. They don't pay any rent, they're the cousins of our landlord, Monsieur Gellé.

I'd rather play with Hélène, our friend on the third floor. She's almost fourteen. When we play, she's the teacher or the mother. My parents' stretching boards propped against the walls become jails for those who misbehave, but those who are good get a piece of her cake. Hélène and Henriette serve tea. I don't disturb them while I'm eating.

My Papa's Arrest

I'm suddenly awakened by loud banging. My heart is pounding. The sound is coming from the back door. It's hardly daylight. I hear Papa ask, "Who's there?"

"Police! Open up! It's the police!"

I'm trembling, hiding behind the curtains. Their feet come thundering up the stairs. They come into the room. I hear a lot of voices talking at once and I make out my father's voice, arguing with them. The officers look mean.

"Why am I being arrested? On what grounds? And by what right? My papers are in order."

The dog barks and Mama picks her up.

"We've been ordered to take you in. Bring the bare necessities and come with us."

"Take me where?" Papa's not letting them push him around.

"Get dressed. Hurry up!"

"It's a mistake!" Papa says, angry.

I'm terrified. Mama puts her hands to her head and mutters, "Oy vey iz mir ... Oy vey iz mir...," over and over. Papa is tight-lipped. He says softly, "It's a mistake, there must be a mistake."

"You're Jewish, aren't you? There's no mistake."

"But I've never made a secret of it! I've declared it, as the government required. I can prove it, I have all the papers."

They prevent him from moving. "Hey! Don't touch anything."

"I need to get my papers." Papa forces his way past them. "Look here. See! 'Voluntary recruit for the duration of the war.' And here's the declaration I spoke of, and my income tax. You can see everything's in order."

The officer interrupts, "You're still a Jew. That's enough. As for

the rest, you'll explain it at the police station. It doesn't concern us." Papa starts to go around the room, gathering his clothes. "Where are you going? Stay here." They follow him. My father replies, "Look, let's be reasonable in front of my family and my little girls. You know I'm not a criminal. I'm a businessman. I have clients. Everyone in the neighbourhood knows me. This doesn't make sense..."

"That's enough! Hurry up or else we'll take you in like this."

Papa answers, "Would you at least have the decency to let me get dressed in private."

"Hurry up, then, instead of standing around talking. This is no time for discussion! Do what you're told instead of creating trouble."

If only I could scream, "Papa is not a troublemaker!" He starts to dress quickly, frowning. Mama has put on her robe and her stockings. Her eyes are wild and I'm frightened. She turns away. With all that's happening, I don't think she sees my sister and me.

I do not feel sleepy anymore. I'm barefoot and shivering. My feet suddenly feel warm... Oh, no! My sister has peed on the floor. I hold my breath, but I feel like shouting.

Papa already has his trousers, shirt and jacket on. He quickly ties the knot of his tie. The officers are watching my parents out of the corners of their eyes. I'm shaking like a leaf. I'm so miserable! Papa ties his shoes and stands up. Adjusting his jacket, he says, "I just need to have a quick wash, if you don't mind."

"Certainly not. Who do you think you are?" They prevent him from going.

"I need to go get my razor. LET ME PASS!"

"Don't make trouble!" shouts the meanest one.

The three of them laugh. Papa takes advantage of the opportunity to open a drawer. One of them grabs his hand. "Okay, that's enough, Éliash! We have others to pick up." Papa pretends he doesn't hear. "Rachel, remember what I'm telling you: the children's certificates of French citizenship are in there. Call Madame Graziani if you need to. Don't worry about me, I won't let the officials push me around." My mother is still wailing, which infuriates me. Papa changes his tone and pleads with them, "Give me a minute with my wife, please."

"Would you like us to play the violin as well?" says an officer, with a smirk.

"There's no time," bellows the third one, already at the door. "We have to get going. He'd take advantage of it to run away. They're sneaky!"

I don't dare move. My legs are numb. You'll be punished! If only Papa had his gun. He's speaking Yiddish now. I don't understand what he's saying. I don't care because the policemen don't understand either. "Enough of that babbling. We're in France here! Get a move on!" shouts an officer, pushing him toward the door. The dog leaps up and bites the lout. The other one gives the dog a kick in the ribs, yelling, "Filthy beast. Down!" Poor Choukette!

Mama croons her "Oy vey iz mir... Oy vey iz mir." What does it mean? "Calm down, Rokheleh! Don't get upset," says Papa. With one shove, they push him out onto the landing. "Let me give my children a kiss!" he demands. My knees are shaking. "They can follow you to number 97, that's where we're meeting."

I know that number, it's Nicolas' house! Papa has put his hat on askew and the collar of his overcoat is turned under. Mama hands him his small suitcase. "Here are a few clothes," she says, sounding distressed. They rush down the stairs. I watch them from the top of the stairs, stunned, and then I follow  Mama to the kitchen window like a sleepwalker. Papa tries to go into the toilet in the courtyard, but they don't let him. They grab him by the arm and drag him like a convict. The concierge finds it funny, watching from her window. She infuriates me!

"See you soon," calls Papa, looking back. My father knows what he's talking about. She'll see, he'll come back! The officers and Papa are walking so fast that by the time we get to the window facing the street, they're already far away. "He didn't even shave and he had nothing to eat," says Mama, upset. Seeing my sister and me, she changes her tone. "Get dressed, girls. We'll go with him."

I've never gotten dressed so fast in my life. Mama has made herself pretty. She's holding a parcel in case Papa needs it. She goes out with Henriette without closing the door. Then she comes back and gets me. She walks very fast and Henriette follows us. When we get outside, they're still there. Phew! We're going to see Papa again! We're still wearing our slippers. He's talking with Dr. David, Dr. Weisman the dentist, Monsieur Salonès and some other people.

"Moisheleh... Moisheleh!" Mama calls. He turns around. He's seen us! I'm so excited! He takes a big step forward. "Stop! Don't move!" says a nasty man.

The three of us walk toward him. With one leap, my sister and I are in his arms. He holds me so tightly I can hardly breathe but I don't get angry. I cling to his body and look hungrily at his face. I won't let him go without me. I kiss him in spite of the bristles of his beard. He looks into my eyes. I'll never let go of him.

What's this racket? A car has just pulled up and the policemen are pointing their guns. "My dear little girls, Henriette and Marguerite,

we have to part now. But it won't be for long. Be good with Mama, don't give her any trouble. Promise?" We nod in agreement.

Someone opens the beautiful gate to the courtyard and they start lining the men up. Papa bends down, releases us from his embrace and sets us both on the ground. I refuse to let go of him. "Come on, children, it's Mama's turn now." I hold on even tighter to him. I'm

the youngest, after all. "You have to let me go. I need to talk to her."
He gives me a gentle push. My mother is crying and he comforts her
instead of me. In my distress, I'm jealous. He takes her tenderly in
his arms. "Calm down, Rokheleh, calm down, please!" They whisper
things into each other's ears.

"We've got everybody. It's time to go, ladies and gentlemen!" The
officers call out the names, one by one, and roughly separate the
women from the men. "David. Éliash. Solanès. Weisman." The men
are packed like sardines into the khaki Citroën. Papa leans out and
shouts, "Courage, Rachel! Courage, children! I'll see you soon!" I'm so
miserable. Mama murmurs under her breath, "Courage, Moishinkeh,
courage!"

I have a stomachache. I have to go home. The cars pull quickly
away. We wave to the one Papa is in as it disappears in the distance.
The sun is rising and with it, my hatred. My heart is so heavy.

We Sleep in Trunks

Later that day, after Papa's arrest,
Madame Dupont, a client of my
parents, takes Henriette and me
to her house. We turn at the corner at the Salvation Army women's
shelter and we walk and walk and walk, very fast! I don't even have
time to look at what we are passing so that I can remember the way. I
pray that we stop soon.

"Number 23!" exclaims Henriette. "Shhh!" says the lady, adding, "Someone might recognize you. That's why I didn't take your mother. We have to take precautions and be very careful because of the arrests." We go up to the third floor and we have something to eat with the lady and her husband. Before we go to bed, she tells us, "You're going to sleep in trunks. If someone comes to the door, I'll close the lids and push them under our bed. Do you understand? Because if the police find you, they will take you away. Okay? Goodnight, children."

She goes back to her husband, who's already snoring. Soon, she's snoring too. It would be better if Mama were here. I can't sleep. I stretch and get up and my sister and I tiptoe to the window. It's dark out but we can see the blue sign of the municipal showers almost right across the street. "There! Do you see that? We're on rue Jules-Vallès, near home. Rue de Charonne is at the end," whispers Henriette. "If they're not nice to us, we'll run away without telling anyone." I change positions ten times before managing to fall asleep.

The next day, we try to leave, but the people grab us by our coat collars and stop us. They scold us, saying, "Honestly, children!" It's dangerous now and we have to be patient and wait. We spend three days playing with their cats before we finally return home.

In the Rain

Mama found a place for us with a kind lady in the country. I eat well and drink as much milk as I want, and the cat lets you pet it. We take turns on the swing under the tree in the yard. The lady never gets angry. When she has a minute, she talks to us. Mademoiselle Aubertin, our violin teacher, came this morning with a parcel full of our clothes from Mama.

The weather is getting cold. The lady writes to Mama to ask for warmer clothes for us. But it's the concierge who answers:

Dear Madame,

Did you know that you do not have the right to keep Jewish children in your home? It is against the law. If you do not return them immediately, I will be forced to report you to the police. It is up to you not to be complicit....

Madame Decuinière

"What should I do?" the lady asks, wiping away tears. She reads us the letter. "I could be convicted because you're in my house! I really don't have a choice." She gets her bicycle out. With Henriette's help,

she puts our clothes in the suitcase, which she attaches to the baggage carrier on the back. She picks up everything else that belongs to us, making sure not to forget anything. She puts it all in a cardboard box, which she places on the handlebars. Wearing our raincoats, we climb on. It's uncomfortable. "I can't do any better," she says, sitting in the middle. The weather is bad and she pedals hard in the wind and the rain and the darkness, oblivious to the late hour.

It's fine with me, I'm not afraid anymore. I'm going back to Mama. We don't meet a single person on the road the whole way. My hands are wet through my gloves and my feet are soaked to the bone.

We get to Paris at sunrise. I'm delighted to be back. "We'll soon be at your house!" says the woman, out of breath. I can't wait to get there. I can hardly keep my eyes open. We stop. Here we are! The concierge is not at her window. Good! Everyone is sleeping. We knock on the door and in seconds my mother is there, taking me, dripping, into her arms. Oh, I'm so happy! The woman doesn't come up. She inflates her tires with the pump and heads off down the street.

That's the last I ever see of her.

The Courtyard of Number 99

Hélène is at her piano, practising. The concierge is watching what's happening from her window. Before putting our garbage cans in the street, she rummages through them and takes whatever she finds, even though my mother passes on our old clothes to her children and

sometimes even gives her food. She's so nosy that Mama gets angry. She wants to know where our mail comes from and who sent it!

The Maillards on the fifth floor have a daughter whose name is also Henriette; she's very nice. We don't see them often. At nightfall, Monsieur Maillard takes their bucket down to the toilet in the court-yard. When it overflows, he yells for the concierge's husband, "Léon! Come unplug the crapper!" But Léon takes his time getting dressed, swearing rudely.

The Pallarès from the fourth floor do the same as Madame Weinstein, the tenant on the third: they knock on his door, shouting, "Please!" Sometimes it smells so bad I have to hold my nose.

On Sunday morning, the plant is closed and so are the stores, except for Madame Hortense's café, which is closed on Monday. All kinds of people go there, even Germans, and women wearing a lot of makeup and not a lot of clothes. I can see them from our house, from the bedroom. I listen to them sometimes; they're funny. There are the drunks she throws out when she's in a bad mood, shouting, "Go sleep it off somewhere!" They say a lot of silly things in Madame's café!

There are also elegant men wearing hats and gloves, like Papa. Mama gives them parcels to take to Drancy. After that, we don't see them again and we find out that my father never received the parcels. The big par-cels, we give to Madame Moireau, a client of my parents, or to Madame Graziani. Unfortunately, Drancy is not in Paris. Papa needs his cologne to wash, and dry sausage and tins of sardines so he  won't die of hunger, and cotton pads and aspirins for his head. Mama is always worrying.

Hopscotch

We're playing hopscotch on the sidewalk, in a spot where Mama can see us. We have plenty of chalk and pencils in the house. I trace the lines and Henriette writes the numbers and names – naturally, she's the one who decides. We use an empty candy tin as a marker. We throw it and hop on one foot, pushing the marker along as we move from one square to the next. We go up to "Home," to squares 7 and 8, and there, with our legs apart, we turn around quickly and go back the other way to square 1, and

then to "Start," which is the only square where you're allowed to rest with both feet together. Then we start again, following the numbers. If you step on a line or if you fall, you lose. But we keep on playing. We start again and try to win next time. We have a lot of fun together when we want to.

Germans on My Street

"Left! Right! Left!" I run as fast as I can and stand just inside the carriage entrance. German soldiers are marching by; it's the war. Some of them aren't looking at anything and some are looking all around them. One of them smiles at me, but I keep away from him. "Left! Right! Left!" The soldiers lift their feet like puppets. Their boots shine in the sun and their steps reverberate in my ears. "Left! Right! Left!" It makes my stomach rumble, and I hurry back into the house.

Dirty Jews!

Now that Papa is gone, things are terrible. Henriette gets angry all the time, Georgette comes less often and Mama doesn't listen to me the way she used to. Choukette misses her master. When I take her out for a pee, I feel like I'm being watched. Everyone gets on my nerves. I walk her when there's nobody around. Someone has scribbled "Dirty Jews" on both our metal shutter and the Bieders'. We've heard that the

Jews we know have had their telephones and radios confiscated. "I'll never let them take the upstairs one!" Mama says.

The next day, she opens the door of the store to a uniformed employee of the Postes, Télégraphes et Téléphones. He cuts the telephone wires in spite of her pleas. "How will I contact my clients? At least leave me the one in the apartment!" He remains deaf to her pleas. He fills out his papers, puts one of them on the desk and leaves the shop with the telephone under his arm, saying, "Now let's go up to the second floor." I go up the stairs fearfully, on tiptoes, and hide at the edge of the kitchen. The employee is in the living room with Mama. I approach them quietly, unnoticed. He does the same thing with the upstairs phone and puts the two telephones in his big bag and throws it over his shoulder. This is really not funny. He smiles, saying, "You may as well close your business, the Jews are going away, as you know." And he leaves, taking our telephones away with him. Mama is crying, her tears falling on the paperwork he gave her. She hasn't locked the door. I am thinking that I won't be able to call Auntie anymore, or Uncle, or answer on the fourth ring.

Everything is awful now. In his last letter, Papa said he hadn't received her parcels, not even the ones brought by our friends, who hadn't been allowed to see him. Where did they go? Why is Papa staying there? I don't understand.

Sitting on the step, Mama moans, "Oy vey iz mir... Oy vey iz mir." Then she suddenly stands up and says, "I'm going to the café. I'll use their phone to let people know what has happened. Come with me?" I answer, "I don't want to. I don't like the drunks. I'd rather stay here."

She locks the door to the shop, goes out the back and runs to the neighbours'. I hate this silence. I can't stand it anymore. I climb heavily up to the landing, cross the big empty room and stand at the window between the half-open shutters.

A woman stops in front of our store. She tries the door, but it's locked. She backs away a little, looks up and shouts, "Is anyone there?"

I make myself as small as possible. She repeats, "Is anyone there?" The whole street is going to know that Mama isn't here. "Madame Élias!" she shouts. I take a deep breath, lean carefully over the window ledge and answer, pointing my finger. "She's next door, over there."

"Be careful you don't fall!" she says.

Then she looks at herself in our mirror, fixes her hair, puts on some lipstick and walks into the bistro. I go listen to the radio.

Madame Graziani has promised to get Papa freed, and it shouldn't be long. We mustn't worry. Soon after they take the phone away, she comes to visit. Her arms full of parcels, she gives the biggest one to Henriette. "It's for the two of you," she says. My sister smiles and then tears off the wrapping. It's a grocery store set, with a scale and weights and a cash register filled with pretend bills. There are cans of food and shelves with bottles of wine and milk and jars of jam and vegetables and fruit. There's even a counter with a drawer. Everything is miniature. We'll be able to play store! "So, do you like it?" asks our generous friend. We thank her very much and give her a kiss.

"That's not all. I have a surprise for Marguerite," she adds with her usual cheerfulness. I open the parcel feverishly. It's a blue telephone, brand new, with a nice ringer.

"Look at this. When you pick up, it makes a click," she explains. "Now, you talk."

I shout, "Hello? Do you hear me?"

"I can hear you. You don't need to yell. You dial VOL 21–40 and wait. Do you understand?"

"Yes, but what if there's no one at the other end of the line?"

She reacts with mock indignation, then demonstrates. "Watch me. 'Hello? Yes? Hello, Uncle. How are you? I have a new telephone. I can say what I want, to whoever I want, when I want, as long as I want!' It's yours, little one, all yours! And if anyone tries to take it away from you, they'll have to answer to me!"

I throw my arms around her neck and hug her

with all my strength. I'm going to call my father right away. She says to my sister, "You have to let her." And then to both of us, "Now I'm going to talk to your Mama. Have fun. Don't fight. I'll see you later." I dial our number VOL 21–40. "Hello, Papa?" I am happy.

After the telephones, they take away our radio. I watch the man unplug it and remove it, ignoring me while I sit there crying. Why take it from us? We pass the time listening to my sister read the newspaper while Mama works and smokes her Gauloises and her Troupes. She has a cloud of smoke around her all day long.

We've moved everything around in the apartment because of our neighbour. Madame Bosch is old and she's meaner than the *Boches*. Every time Mama uses the sewing machine, she bangs on the wall with her wooden leg. The corner where we used to sleep is now the workshop. The downstairs is closed and we're not allowed to go there anymore. Uncle moved the furniture from the dining room to the living room. He put nice wallpaper with roses on it around the beds in our new bedroom. I rest there and play store. The room is smaller, but it's above our shop and there's less noise than above the bistro. If only I could listen to the radio! The tailor and the shoemaker have gone away. Papa hasn't come back. I can't stand this.

The Black Market

At nightfall, the travelling grocer comes on his tricycle to deliver the things we ordered the week before. He's nice to us when we give him money. Our old customers bring us their furs to repair, very late at night. This is called the black market. We aren't supposed to talk about it.

André, the worker we had before the Germans came, also brings work for our mother. He arrives very early in the morning and picks up the finished work the next day. Mama only stops to eat and sleep.

She doesn't have time to talk or laugh with us. No more funny stories for us to listen to. No more news to discuss. No more romantic songs, no more music – except the violin.

I'm a bird in a cage. I can be a perfect angel, but there's nobody to praise me for it anymore. But Papa is going to come back, Madame Graziani says so. He should be back before my birthday, I tell my dolls. Oh, if only they could talk!

December 4, 1941 – I Turn Five

The first star is shining in a huge, dark sky. It's the last chance for Papa to come before the end of the day. I wait with my nose against the icy window in the kitchen. I'm losing hope that he'll come tonight. In the courtyard, night has fallen. But when I see the silhouette of a man moving slowly outside, I tremble with joy.

Henriette is reading the news out loud to Mama, who's finishing the merchandise she has to deliver to the mean managing commissioner. In the dim light of the workshop, I get a better view of the man passing by. I'm terribly disappointed – it's an old man holding a package tied with a ribbon. But he seems to be looking for something. When he reaches our door, he knocks – one knock, two knocks, three knocks. I tiptoe to the landing. He keeps knocking. We're reluctant to open the door. "Just because it's the war doesn't mean you have to alert the whole city!" Mama mumbles and finally decides to open the door. "Monsieur Salonès! You frightened us! What are you doing out at this hour?" she says in a whisper, happy to see the old man back from Drancy.

"I beg your pardon, Madame. Your husband asked me to give this to you." He holds out the package, adding, "It's for the little one, the one called Marguerite." I'm choked up with happiness and sadness at the same time.

"Thank you for going to the trouble. You're a good man. If there's anything I can do to return the favour, don't hesitate to give me a

call. No, I forgot, that's impossible... let me know. How can I thank you? I'll give this to my daughter right away. Good night!"

She locks the door and turns around. Seeing me standing there at the top of the stairs, she comes upstairs, shouting, "Margueriteleh! I have a present for you!" as if I didn't already know.

I grab the package from her hands and hold it close. I go behind the curtains, thinking, last year he was here, standing in front of my cake with four lit candles on it, smiling at me in the dark. He had scolded Henriette who, for once, wasn't the favourite. "Let her blow out the candles all by herself," he had said, pushing her gently. He had taken me onto his lap in his armchair and given me a kiss for each year of my age, plus one for the next year.

Even though he couldn't be here with us this year, he had thought of me! I untie the bow and tear off the paper. Inside is a beautiful round box of candy with flowers on it. I take off the cover of the box and it's filled with delicious chocolates wrapped in papers of different colours. I'm laughing and crying with joy mixed with pain, and I call to my sister and my mother, "Come see!" The three of us sit down with a pho-

tograph of Papa. Mama lights the candle beside Papa's picture and eats a chocolate to Papa's health. My sister does the same. "To your health, Papa!" I eat mine slowly, savouring them, while they go back downstairs to finish the order. I pick up my telephone and call. "Hello, Papa? I have good news for you. I got your parcel. Thank you!"

Today, I'm five years old.

In German Hands

The sun has just come up. Finally, it's going to be a nice day! With my box of chocolates, I'm in heaven. Mama is emptying our garbage

in the garbage cans in the court-yard across from the big gate and without asking her, I run outside. A man in a grey-green uniform catches me around the waist, laughing. "Uh, uh, uh!" he says, picking me up off the ground. He's a German! There are three of them and they won't stop laughing. I want to shout, "Let go of me! I have to go home!" but I can't say anything. Dangling there like a fish at the end of a line, I wriggle. He holds on to me. He's so powerful and I'm so small. The three soldiers look at me strangely, talking in their gibberish that I don't understand.

Suddenly, the one with the sparkling teeth and the moustache like Hitler exclaims, "A real little *Mädchen!*" and sets me down on the ground without completely letting go of me. He adds in a soft voice, "You see, I am not so bad! It is true, no?"

I don't wait a second. I run away and find myself clinging to Mama with my head against her belly, whimpering. She picks me up like a sack of laundry and carries me into the house. She climbs the stairs, throws me on my bed and, completely out of breath, stammers, "Do you understand now?" I bow my head and say, "Yes, Mama."

Hello? Hello?

When I'm bored, I call Papa, Madame Graziani or Auntie Sonia. If I don't know their numbers, I just dial 0. It's impossible to hear them, but I know they're listening and nobody interrupts me. By myself in

the bedroom, in the glow from the street light, I dial VOL taire 21–40. When I run out of news to tell them, I just make things up. With my blue telephone, I say whatever I want, to whomever I want, whenever I want.

Saint-Bernard School

I go to school on rue Saint-Bernard, right beside Sainte-Marguerite church. I never get there late, although I'm the smallest. The teacher is a customer of ours. She wears her mink stole around her neck with a matching hat and always smiles at me. She put a book on my chair so I can reach the desk, which is too high for me. She teaches us the music notes, using the piano to sing "Do, re, mi, fa, so, la, ti, do." She accompanies us when we sing. I don't always know the right words and I sing "I'm a little teapot short and stout, here is my handle, here is my mouth...."

We draw, we colour, we count on our fingers and, sometimes, if we're good, she gives us pictures. If we're extra good, she gives us treats. Was she ever surprised when she found out I already knew the alphabet! And that I could recite the whole thing! She's teaching us to read and write.

On my notebook, she wrote, "Perfect!" I was the first one to spell out my name, MARGUERITE, with little sticks. In front of all the girls, she pinned a merit badge on my jacket. I was so proud. I like it when people admire my badge. When I move, the lovely red ribbon shines. But when I show it to my sister, she laughs at me. "It's kindergarten, it doesn't count!" And to think that I have to stay at the door with her and wait for Georgette to pick us up at noon! When we walk on the sidewalk, everyone notices my badge. When we get back home, I look at myself in the mirror at the store, with the mannequins. And truly, it's even more beautiful in the light! My mother will be so happy! I'm so impatient for her to come back, I can't stand it. Finally, I hear her key in the lock. "Mama! Mama! Look what I won!"

The Thief

"Give me back the black pencil you took from me," I say to Yvette. The other girls don't believe me, but I insist. "What's going on here?" asks the teacher when she walks into the classroom. I tell on Yvette. "She's hiding my things in her drawer!" Madame Petit opens the drawer and looks at the name on the pencil. She sees that it's mine and gives it to me along with the eraser I thought I'd lost. Then she hits Yvette's hands with her metal ruler. It must hurt because Yvette winces. "Let this be a lesson to you never to steal or lie!"

As soon as the teacher turns her head away, Yvette mutters, "Just you wait! I'll get you for this. You'll be sorry." She really hates me. "It's your fault!" she shouts. "No!" I protest. And then she's standing in the corner with her face to the wall for calling me a liar.

The next day, her father comes to school with her. That nasty man scares me. Luckily, the teacher is waiting at the door, watching us out of the corner of her eye. "You're nothing but a dirty little Yid! Riff-raff!" he says to me. Everyone hears him! Everyone is laughing! The girls are whispering to each other. What does he mean? If only I could disappear...

My schoolbag is heavy with my paintbox, my pencil case, my slate and my chalkboard eraser, my book and my exercise books. My sister's is even worse. But in spite of that, we have to hold hands when we cross the street. I can't wait until Papa comes back so he can take us to school.

The Siren

A shrill wailing sound tears me from sleep. It rises higher and high-er, louder and louder, and goes down softer and softer, and then begins again. It makes everything from floor to ceiling vibrate. I tremble and snuggle down in my bed. Through the slats of the shutters, the light from the street lamp traces lines on the wall. Henriette's striped silhouette is immobile, frozen in fear.

The door opens and there's Mama, already dressed to go out. "Quickly, children! It's an air raid siren! There's not a minute to lose! We have to go down to the shelter." She shakes my sister and throws some clothes at her. Then she dresses me from head to toe. We hurry. I take a doll and my pillow, and Henriette takes her pillow and her schoolbag full of books. Mama follows us, laden with a bag of food, her knitting, her sewing, a blanket and a hatbox. I'm the first one on the stairs. I cross the courtyard to the sidewalk. Madame Hortense is staring up at the sky, counting the black specks flying above, and doesn't notice me. I don't even say hello because I'm running. Here we are at the entrance to the shelter. We're all emotional – this is where we hugged Papa the day he was arrested!

There are a lot of women and children blocking the entrance to the shelter, but fewer men because of the camps. We take our place

in the line – all that rushing just to stand here waiting. More people line up behind us. Everyone is pushing and shoving, and I feel like I'm going to be crushed. Mama stretches her arm out in front of an old gentleman who has gotten between her and me, and asks, "Would you mind letting my children pass?" He motions us to go ahead of him. "And what about ours, can't they get in?" shouts the concierge on my right, adding, "Foreigners have all the rights." What is she talking about? I'm French!

"Move, move!" people shout. "Shut up!" replies an angry voice, "There's no point pushing." A low drone is heard overhead and quiets the crowd. Now we're moving. The fear of air raids pushes us forward. Phew! It's about time!

"I can't see anything. I can't breathe," I say, loudly enough for everyone to hear me. Mama scolds me. "You're not a baby. You can see my hands are full!" The light goes out just when I'm about to enter the tunnel leading to the basement. "Mama! Mama!" I cry, blinded. "It's all right, sweetie. Do you want to get up on my shoulders?" asks the funny old fellow from before. I climb up as best I can. People complain because we've stopped for a minute. It isn't easy, with my doll and my pillow. But now I can see everything, although I have to be careful not to hit my head. "Aren't you the furriers? My wife was a client of yours. She was very pleased with your work," he says. I cling more closely to him. I remember the times I rode on Papa's shoulders like this. Closing my eyes, I imagine he's Papa.

We walk slowly until we find a place on the ground. In this room, with its stone walls, it's cold on the blanket. We share our meal by candlelight with my benefactor. Henriette reads in the dim light,

Mama knits something for Papa, and my thoughts drift to Drancy, where he's interned.

Locked in the Toilet

The teacher has explained that we are to go to the bathroom during recess, that if we go during class, disturbing the other students, she'll be angry and we'll be punished by having to stand in the corner or stay after school. I've never been punished. These are squat toilets and when we pull the chain to flush, we can easily get our feet wet. I have a system, though: before pulling the chain, I lift the latch on the door so that I can get out quickly and avoid the problem.

I perform this feat... Standing on tiptoe, I reach out, grab the end of the chain, give it a quick pull and run. "Ow, ow, ow!" I've hit my head on the door and now my feet are wet. I don't understand why the door didn't open. "Is anyone there?" I call, but no one answers.

The bell rings. We have to line up to go back into class. I wish I hadn't gone to the bathroom so late. I'll have to.... "Silence!" I hear the principal's voice say, as if she were speaking right to me. I can't bang on the door without being noticed. So I push with all my might. But it doesn't give. I stand on my tiptoes and try to grip the top of the door with my fingers, but I can't reach, I'm too short. "Not another sound, please! Form a line, two by two, and no talking!" orders the principal. She acts like the police, making the students line up with their hands behind their backs, their eyes looking down, without saying a word. She's very strict.

And am I supposed to keep quiet? One class goes back in. I have a stomachache. And then another class… I have diarrhea. Finally, the last class moves forward. I've finished. How can I get out of here? I'm shaking all over. I imagine the students walking quietly and as they move away, I feel a pain growing in my chest and I'm overcome with fear. There's no one in the yard now. Nobody but me here. Are they going to leave me in this place until school lets out?

I put my ear up to the door. I hear the rustling of leaves in the wind. I'm going to have to get out of here, but how? What if I lay on the ground and tried to get under the door? That's it! I get down on the ground but I can't get under the door, and now I'm all dirty. It's disgusting. I stink now. Yvette will be right to say that I'm dirty! I hold my nose. I can't stand it! I decide to shout, "Help! Please! I'm locked in the toilet. Help me get out! Please, get me out!"

All I hear in the huge schoolyard is silence. I'm in prison, but why? Come on, I mustn't give up! I'll sing, I'll sing so loud that I'll be heard at the ends of the earth!

Au clair de la lune,
Mon ami Pierrot,
Prête-moi ta plume,
Pour écrire un mot.
Ma chandelle est morte,
Je n'ai plus de feu,
Ouvre-moi ta porte,
Pour l'amour de Dieu!

I really put my heart into singing the last line. "Open the door, for the love of God!" I shout. "Do you hear me? Do you hear me? Open the door! Please, someone, open the door, for the love of God!"

Poor little girl, there's no use singing your heart out. I listen to the water gurgling from the pipe and the beating of a bird's wings as it soars into the sky. Salty tears are trickling into my mouth and my nose is running. I take my beautiful embroidered handkerchief and wipe my nose. Everyone has abandoned me like Hansel and Gretel in the story, except I'm all alone and I'm not in the forest. I don't need a trail of bread crumbs to find my way – all I need is for someone to come and let me out. I have been crouching down for so long that my legs are numb and my feet are tingling. If only I were bigger!

My tears make me want to pee again, but I don't pull the chain this time. The walls are covered with scribbling and there are brown fingerprints. There's a rusty nail holding torn-up pieces of newspaper for wiping yourself. The writing is all blurred. I feel like I'm going to fall in the dark hole of the toilet. I think I hear the big bad wolf coming... he smells my tender flesh. I put my head down between my knees in the middle of all the filth. It's dark.

I hear a sound. Someone is coming. I don't dare budge. "Which one is she in?" It's my teacher! "I think it's that one," my friend Colette answers timidly. My friend! I call, "Here I am. I'm here!" The door opens. I stand up quickly. Madame Petit stretches her arms out to me and holds me as if she were my Mama. She takes me back to the classroom and has me sit at my desk. I fall asleep.

The bell rings. Madame Petit gathers my things and puts them in my schoolbag. Mama is waiting at the door of the school. She and my teacher are talking. Henriette starts pestering me with questions. "Is it true they locked you in? Tell me what happened." I don't feel like talking, I wish she'd be quiet.

My teacher shakes hands with Mama and gives me a hug. She says to Mama, "Dear Madame Élias, I'm terribly sorry, but I don't see any other way. As for you, Marguerite, forget about this incident. Keep on studying during this forced vacation. And good luck! I'll see you soon!"

We walk away very fast. We go back home without speaking and then, as if we were starving, we eat half a cake for our snack. I keep trying to figure out why I couldn't get out. And why should I be punished by not being allowed to go to school?

Jews can't have telephones or radios anymore and they can't go to the movies or the park. Mama is going to "rent a grandfather" who'll take us to play in the park. For now, the only thing I can do is walk the dog.

In the Luxembourg Gardens with "Grandpa"

It's beautiful out today. I feed the birds the breadcrumbs I saved in my napkin this morning. The last "grandpa" complained that we were too well dressed in comparison to him. Mama gave him a suit of Papa's

to wear, but he gave it back. He won't be coming again; it's too risky. He was so nice to me. The new one she found for us buys us each a balloon with our money. They're floating above our heads. Henriette took the blue one I wanted, so mine is yellow. It's true it's the colour of the sun, but it's not the same.

"Grandpa" has me sitting on a chair, but it's not a good place for watching the pigeons pecking on the ground. "Take a look at those uniforms," he mutters, pretending to wipe his nose with his hand-

kerchief. German words echo in the icy silence. There's a whole group of soldiers. Hiding his face behind his newspaper, "Grandpa" says in a low voice, "We have to look normal so that they won't notice us. Just walk away quietly as if they weren't there." He picks up his socks and shoes, which he had taken off when we got to the park, and puts them back on. He takes me by the hand and whispers to us, "Don't look back along the way. You'll soon be back home."

We leave the park and cross the street to where they won't see us and we go into the métro station. We don't say a word all the way to our door. When we get home, Mama pays him and whispers something to him, ignoring us, and then he goes away. "He didn't stay as long, but he wanted more money," Mama complains. I tell her what happened but she doesn't listen to me; she has no patience for it.

She sits down at the machine and sews without stopping. If we disturb her, she scolds us and sends us to the kitchen to do our homework. But what's the point if the teacher can't see it? The butt of her cigarette is hanging pitifully from her lips, and she takes another one. She holds the butt to it and inhales deeply to make it light. She says to us, "I'm sorry, children, but I have to

deliver this before the end of the day. I'm running late. You'll have to find something to do because I have to work. I'll see you later, young ladies." Like a locomotive going full speed, she starts sewing again.

On the Swings with Georgette

Georgette comes every morning and brings fresh bread and milk. She goes through the café and uses our back door to avoid being seen by the concierge, Madame Decuinière. She makes breakfast while Mama  works downstairs in the work-shop. Then she takes us to the small park on rue Saint-Bernard where I used to go to school. She's our maid, but she's a friend.

"Step on it, Marguerite! Come on, girls, step on it!" She's always in a hurry. She's very strong. She can carry me in her arms and swing me in the air. I'm not afraid of her. When I won the merit badge, she shouted for joy. And she made a cake fit for a queen especially for me. I gobbled it up and got it all over me. She showed me my face in the mirror and we laughed, and then she washed my face.

Nobody dares bother us when she's with us. She mends our things and knits pullovers and skirts without letting us out of her sight. She pushes us both on the swings at one time. There are other adults who try to do that, but they can't do it as fast or as long as she can. When we see other children with their schoolbags, we shout out in unison, "Again! Higher!" but the truth is that we feel like undesirables.

The Salvation Army Women's Shelter

A few steps from our house, at the corner of rue Faidherbe, is the Salvation Army women's shelter. It's open to people passing by. I know lots of women who live there. As the name indicates, it isn't for men and there are hardly any there. It's an army that works for God and helps the poor and unfortunate. I sometimes see them outside, telling their stories. They are against war and all misery. From our

windows over the shop, I can see the right-hand side of their building. It's the tallest building in the neighbourhood.

Late one afternoon during the curfew, when everyone is going home, a woman lieutenant comes to get my sister and me in spite of the law. She's one of our customers, a woman officer. I like her hat with red ribbons and her blue uniform. She takes us by the hand and we go with her to their Christmas party. I'm proud to walk with her, even though I'm particularly afraid because it is dangerous for us to be out at this time. But I feel protected. Mama is right when she says they do "good works."

There are a lot of children there in a huge room. There are white tablecloths on the tables. After a speech about the birth of baby Jesus, loving thy neighbour and tolerance, the ladies give us each a glass of lemonade. And then we all rush for the loot bags that are filled with treats – candies, cookies, a little chocolate bar for Henriette and lollipops for me. We sing songs accompanied by accordion, violin and piano. I love the last song, "Oh night, how deep your silence, when the golden stars sparkle in the heavens." It's so soft and beautiful that it makes me sleepy.

We leave with bigger smiles than when we arrived. We're the only ones in the street when the lieutenant takes us back. I'm happy and give her a big hug. She hugs us and rushes away, saying, "May God be with you!"

The Yellow Star

Mama has received a package of stars made of yellow fabric, which she sews on our clothes, right where I had my merit badge. This one is ugly. What a horrible colour!

Henriette begs for me to have one too – I don't have to wear it since I'm only five and a half. But she insists or else she won't wear one either. "If you don't have one, you'll go to prison! All by yourself! They'll lock you up in the toilet again. They'll make you stand in the corner!" she says, making up things to persuade me.

I complain to my mother, "Tell her it isn't true!" Mama finally notices me and puts down the garment she's holding saying, "I'm sorry, dear, but you know, she's not completely wrong. We have to wear the star for now, until all this is over. It can't last long. Here, this is yours,

go put it away." She hands me the sweater and I put it on to look at myself in it.

"It's the law!" my sister shouts, just to annoy me. "If you don't understand, it's because you want to be a baby!" She keeps repeating it.

"What is the law?"

"It's what people have to do."

"Not me. I don't have to do anything."

"You're not the one who decides! And you're almost as big as I am!"

"Don't be so hard on your little sister, dear, try to be nice to her. Why don't you read us the news?"

Taking advantage of the fact that they're busy, I tiptoe out and go

down to the shop to look at myself in the three-way mirror. The star is even uglier in the mirror. All this because of the *Boches*! We're not allowed to put the heat on downstairs and it's colder there. I listen to the sounds of the street. I'd rather be upstairs.

I go up to my room and telephone Papa. I hope he'll hear me this time. "Hello, Papa? It's me. Henriette is whining. She says they'll point at her at school. I don't care about them, because they don't want me."

Uh oh, here comes my sister. I take off my sweater, which I suddenly hate. She grabs me. "What are you doing?"

"I want to be Catholic!" I say.

Now that we're wearing the star, everyone looks at us. In the street, people stare at us like monkeys at the zoo. People I like turn their backs on me now. Except for Hélène. She sewed her stars on by herself. She showed us her beautiful new dress that they bought her for the piano

recital she'll soon be giving. The three of us are invited to it and it will be my first time going to a recital. "If the Germans come to get us, I'll wear my new dress!" she said defiantly. Her mother, suddenly angry, said, "Shut up, you little idiot, you don't know what you're saying."

I want to stick my tongue out

at everyone. But I hate being scolded, so I wait until we get home and then really stick it out.

They Take Hélène and Her Mama Away

One week later, at sunrise, there are three knocks on our door. It's not a nightmare. It's someone we know. Maybe it's Papa! I can't control my excitement. I jump out of bed and run across the kitchen to the landing. "Stay there!" cries Mama, rushing down the stairs. In a low voice, she asks, "Who's there?"

"It's Madame Weinstein, Madame Élias! Open up, hurry!" It's the neighbour on the third floor, with her daughter, Hélène. I'm cold and huddle in my nightgown.

"What do you want at this hour?" asks Mama, surprised.

They speak in their foreign language. But I see the suitcase and I guess what it's about. Hélène has kept her promise – she's put on her new dress. "Goodbye, Henriette! Goodbye, Marguerite!" she cries, holding her schoolbag.

"Leave, please, I'm begging you!" says Mama.

"Auf Wiedersehen," answers Madame Weinstein, and adds confidentially, "They don't know who you are, I haven't said anything."

My mother slams the door in their faces, stammering, "Goodbye! Good luck to you, too!" And then she comes back up and collapses on the bed.

Goodbye, Hélène. I won't hear her piano anymore or go to her recital. I feel a great sorrow rising in me.

Voltaire Métro Station

We take the métro to the dentist. I have a terrible toothache in one of my big teeth. We have to wait a long time for the train and I can't stop

crying from the pain. Mama begs me to be quiet, but my tooth hurts so much. We get off at République and walk very fast.

The dentist is also wearing a yellow star. He takes me before the other patients. "Come in, little one. I'll take care of this for you," he says kindly. He seats me in the chair and asks me to open my mouth. He picks up a small pair of pliers.

I can't see what he does, but I feel it. "Ow, ow, ow!" I cry, clinging to my mother, who is preventing me from moving. "Ow, ow, ow!
Stop! Stop!"

"I'm almost done. Just a bit more. There, that's it!" he says. His
hands are covered in blood. Oh, he's so mean!

He washes the tooth off and gives it to me, saying, "Put it under
your pillow and the Little Mouse will put a present in its place. Isn't
that true, Madame Élias?" I rinse my mouth and he puts a big wad
of cotton in the hole. Looking at his watch, he says, "Hurry up, it will
soon be curfew."

Mama pays him and we rush off into the métro. Even Henriette
feels sorry for me. She strokes my hand. Everyone looks at our stars,
which makes me feel even worse.

The Food Line

Mama does her shopping quickly. She cannot leave the house earlier than three o'clock and has to be back before curfew at four. As soon as I see her pick up her purse, I hurry to get ready because I like to go with her. I enjoy it when it is just the two of us.

While she waits in line, I make up games. I count hats, gloves and things made of fur. I walk on the sidewalk, jumping over the cracks instead of stepping on them because if I do, I lose. I go to the corner of the street and then turn around. I do this almost every day. We have to be home at four o'clock, not a minute later! No wandering around the neighbourhood.

In the Gutter

I go with Mama to buy a few groceries. She comes out of the grocery store at the corner of rue de la Cité and passes me, calling, "I'm going to run over to the other bakery. Be careful!" I'm always careful.

She's already far ahead of me. I move slowly, quietly counting my steps. "One... two... three...." By the time I get to ten, she's completely disappeared from view. Ten more and she'll be back. I start counting again in front of the florist's shop. "One... two... three... four...."

The florist's daughters shout insults at me. Then they grab me, yelling, "Get lost! Get the hell out of here, dirty Yid!" They push me into the gutter and run back inside. I fall flat in the filthy water. My mouth is full of it and so are my nose and my ears. It's disgusting. I'm drowning in it.

"Mar-gue-rite!" My mother is calling me. When she finds me, she takes me in her arms and says over and over, "My poor little girl! My poor little girl!" I'm drenched to the bone. She hugs me to her. The water trickles into my shoes. I press against her, crying and trembling, asking, "Why, Mama, why?"

They Take Mama Away

Someone knocks on our door. Who could it be at this hour? More
and more knocking. My sister, her body striped with the street light
filtering through the shutters, cries frantically, "They've come to get
us!" With one leap, we're up. Choukette is barking. This time, we shut
her in our bedroom. We go through the kitchen and stop at the land-

ing. My heart is pounding in my chest! Mama is petrified. We hang
on to her.

"Open up! Police! Police! Open up!" they
shout. I hide in the folds of my mother's nightgown. They're knocking so hard that the door is
shaking.

My mother calls, "Coming!" and goes down
the stairs. My teeth are chattering, and I shrink
back closer to Henriette. I'm so afraid. Mama
comes back up, surrounded by men. I count them
to myself – there are three of them, the same as with Papa.

"Take the bare minimum, Madame Élias, and follow us to the station," orders the first officer, reading a paper. My feet are frozen. The
second one turns to us and says, "What are you waiting for? Do you
want us to take you in your pyjamas? They said children too!" I really
need to pee. I cross my legs. The third one asks, "What does it take to
make you understand? Don't you speak French?" Henriette runs into
the bedroom. Mama begs them, "Please! They're French nationals.
Here's proof."

"All right then, we won't take the children. But you hurry up!" the
officer says, while she gets dressed in front of them. It's shameful.

Papa was right – you had to show them proof of nationality.
Because of that, we'll stay at home. I would rather go with Mama, but
I don't dare speak up. I stand there like a statue. Mama adds, "I have
to go to the café and telephone someone to take care of them. They're
just six and eight years old."

"Not now. You'll call from there. And we don't
have time for any long goodbyes!" She takes us
in her arms and kisses us, saying in a low voice,
"Be good until I come back. Don't open the
door to anyone you don't like. Lock it behind
me. And above all, don't fight. I'm going to contact Madame Graziani. Go back to your beds,

my sweet little girls. Be good." She looks at Henriette, who's already dressed, and starts to cry.

"We've got to go now!" orders the officer impatiently, leading the way. The others follow him. I can't hear what they're saying anymore.

She's gone away with them, leaving the two of us lost and helpless. From the window over the courtyard, we can see them turn the corner. We rush to the window overlooking the street. They're disappearing. We obey our mother and go back to bed without even looking for something to eat. But I can't sleep because of the officers. Then the alarm clock goes off. It gives me the shivers.

"It's seven o'clock," announces Henriette, getting up and going to the window. The darkness frightens me. We look out between the slats of the shutters so we can't be seen. There's nobody in sight. The silence worries me. What should we do? I'm afraid. I'm cold. I'm hungry. My sister is only interested in her book.

"I'm hungry!" I say, getting out of bed.

"Have some bread and jam," she says.

I decide to go and eat with Choukette.

"Where are you going? Wait for me! I'm the one who decides!"

"Then hurry up. I'm starving!"

"Where are the cookies. Do you see them?"

I show her the package. She opens it and asks, "How many do you want?"

"One, with milk." She gives it to me and then gobbles up a whole bunch herself while I nibble on mine.

"Hey, take it easy," I protest. "You'll finish them!"

"Help yourself," she retorts. "Nobody's stopping you!"

"I'll tell Mama!"

"Okay. Go tell her!" Then she thinks for a minute. "All right, we'll share them half and half." But she cheats again. Her pile is higher.

"You took too many," I say.

She bursts into tears and I feel sorry. I pick up my telephone to call Papa, but she starts laughing at me. I go sit on my bed and slowly dial the number. "Hello, Papa? It's me. They came and took Mama. Henriette is bossing me around!"

"You're talking as if he could hear you!" she interrupts. "Everyone knows it's a toy. Everyone but you!"

"That isn't true!"

"What isn't true? That it's a toy or that you don't know the difference?"

Nobody comes to my defence. Now we're both crying. Henriette paces up and down. I decide to call Papa back.

"Stop that ringing! The concierge will hear!"

"All right, I'll stop it from ringing."

"Do you really think he hears you?"

I don't answer. She tells me I'm a big fat goose. I ask, "What do you mean? I'd really like to know."

"As fat as this," she says, spreading her arms wide. Then she puts them around me and says, "I hope Mama comes back soon." We know that Madame Weinstein and Hélène haven't come back.

We sit down back to back. I try to play with my dolls. Henriette reads out loud. Then we hold each other. She takes stock of the situation. "Auntie Sonia is on vacation. Georgette may be at the café, but we can't go there or call her. André should come and bring work. The managing commissioner is coming Monday. Someone will be coming to pick up the parcel for Papa. Uncle Léon has been in the army since the beginning of the war. Auntie Rose is in the free zone." She buries herself in her book again.

"And where is Mama?" I ask her. "With the Germans?"

"Shh. Someone's at the door!"

We rush to the window. It's a big woman, a customer. She looks angry. We don't open the door and she finally goes away. To please Mama, I get dressed carefully.

Who'll make us lunch? It's already two o'clock and there's been no word from Madame Graziani.

"If the police come to get us, what will we do?" I ask, worried.

"We'll hide until Mama comes back and we'll only leave if people we like come and get us."

"Where will we hide?"

"Behind the double drapes, but we'll have to hold our breath and be very still."

"What if they open the drapes so they can see better?"

"They wouldn't. They'd turn the light on."

"I'd rather hide under my bed."

"That's the worst place! I always find you when you hide there."

"How about under the sink?"

"No, it smells bad."

"Behind the sofa, then. There's enough room."

"That's a good place! Let's try it," my sister says. We crawl in.

After a little while, it's uncomfortable and our legs start to hurt. We come out all dirty and wash up a bit. Choukette is pining for her masters. Henriette gives her some of the milk.

"Not too much. I'm thirsty too!"

"Finish it, then. After that, we'll drink water."

We go back to the window. The concierge is distributing the mail. Maybe there will be a letter for us. But she doesn't come to our door.

"Quiet! I heard the gate close, maybe it's Mama coming back. No, it's the Maillards."

We go have a look at the street. Henriette reaches the window first.

"Germans! Germans as far as I can see. Come look!" cries my sister anxiously.

"You're crazy! They'll hear you all the way to the end of the street!"

"There are lots of Jews with the star, women and children. There's even a girl from my class, do you see her?"

We get into our beds with our clothes on, trembling with fear.

"Stay with me. What if Mama went to be with Papa? It's already four o'clock," my sister says, crying.

There are sounds from the courtyard. There's a drunk talking to the concierge. The toilets must be blocked. He complains, "You can't take a shit here." Henriette goes back to her book, *Sleeping Beauty*. It's more interesting than the paper, but waiting is still hard.

When we wake up, Mama still isn't back. It's hard without a real telephone or a radio, but it's much harder without parents. We cry. The bell rings at Monsieur Gellé's factory – the workers are leaving. It's seven o'clock. We eat some camembert and crackers and the rest of the fruit compote.

We're all grubby from crying. It's dark outside. We don't turn on the light because *they* might see us. Luckily, there's the street lamp in front of our house. We're cold. We put on our fur coats. There's no food left. Choukette barks. "Shh. Quiet!" There's the sound of a key in the lock. We rush to the window. If only it's Mama! We run down the stairs. It's her! "Mama! Mama!" we both cry.

She's very red, her face... She sits down on the bottom step of the stairs and bursts into sobs. She throws her coat into the workshop and stands against the wall. She's crying and singing bits of strange songs and muttering to herself. We beg her to stop, but it's as if we weren't there. What's the matter with her? We sit down beside her and we all cry together. The fur of our coats is all wet with our tears. I want her to talk to us but she clasps her hands and remains mute.

Suddenly she cries out, "They beat me, the swine! They beat me, Moishinkeh! They beat me for slipping a little note into the pocket of an eleven-year-old child. And those who did it, Moishinkeh, they were French! Yes, Moishinkeh! They beat me and I'll never forget it!"

Baptismal Certificates

Mama is in the shop with Madame Binet to give her a fur collar. Sitting on the stairs, I listen attentively to their conversation.

"I need to be able to prove that the girls are Catholic, that they've been baptized. Do you understand?"

"Consider it done. You'll have the papers."

Madame Binet leaves with her gift under her arm. She comes back the next day with an envelope. My mother hardly has time to thank her before she goes away again.

When she comes back the next day, Mama announces, "Madame Binet, I'm very sorry, but the papers don't seem to be good." And she begins to sob.

Madame Binet doesn't understand. She says she'll try to fix it. With tears in her eyes, Mama accompanies her to the door. Madame Binet doesn't look pleased. "I'll do what I can," she reassures our mother.

Early in the morning, the two of them meet again in the corner of the workshop.

"This time, they're good, Madame Élias. I got them from a parish priest."

"How much do I owe you? And this is just between us, of course," Mama adds. Holding out a wad of bills, she asks, "Is this enough?" Madame Binet slips the bills into her wallet without counting them.

Mama takes a paper bag and puts a nice piece of fur trim in it. "Take this, it's for you, to wear around your neck or on your head." After they exchange thanks, Madame Binet leaves, saying, "These ones will be fine, I assure you."

We Throw Away the Stars

Mama has a long conversation with us. She explains how she was freed thanks to Madame Graziani. Then she says that Henriette and I have to leave home without her. The government is arresting all the Jews in Paris, even the ones who are French. We can't stay here anymore. She reminds us of when we went away to Fontainebleau, the time we spent without her in the country with the lady who brought us back on her bicycle because the concierge had informed on us, and of Hélène's arrest. She tells us the story of the Virgin and baby Jesus because we are going to pretend to be Catholics. We will have to pretend until the war ends and Papa comes back. We have to hide separately from her. I listen closely without understanding. While she speaks, she cuts the threads from the stars and removes them from our clothes. I take them and throw them in the air, laughing. "They fly, Mama! Look at my shooting stars!"

I'm happy. We laugh for a minute and then she takes us in her arms and kisses us tenderly. She looks at the time and says, "Time to go to bed, girls. It's midnight. I have a lot of things to get ready." We go to bed sadly. How is the separation going to happen? She says goodnight and turns off the light.

"Leave the door open, please!" Henriette begs her.

What did Mama mean? It's keeping me awake. Where will we go? Who will take us? We get out of our beds and tiptoe over to watch her. She fills her hatbox with the best merchandise. She puts our clothes in our suitcase and then changes some of them for others. She places some photographs and all sorts of papers inside the big picture frame that she's taken down from the wall. She throws a lot of things in the garbage. She wraps her big gold spoon in a black cloth and puts it in the bottom of her shoulder bag. Nobody must know that I went with her to the jeweller's to have her rings and necklace and our chains and bracelets melted down. Then she sits down at the corner of the table where she used to eat with Papa and puts her face down on her arms, wailing, "Oy vey iz mir…" Without a word to each other, my sister and I go back to our beds. The sandman comes and I fall asleep.

The Great Departure

We wake up at dawn. There's no hot water for us to wash but it doesn't matter – we don't have time. We put on our best outfits, white fur coats and hats. My sister brings her violin. I bring my baby doll, which is the least heavy of my dolls. I can't bring the stroller or my pedal car or any other toys.

"Are you ready, girls?" asks Mama tearfully from the kitchen. She hasn't stopped wailing and shouting. Now, she opens the sideboard and takes out some crystal glasses. She throws them against the wall we share with the neighbours, saying something I don't understand. Crash, bang! The neighbour answers by knocking on the wall with her crutch, once, twice, three times. "Stop it, Mama! Stop!" begs my sister. Everything is so painful right now.

A short woman arrives. "She's a dwarf," my sister whispers in my ear with a mischievous smile. She's going to take us to her daughter who has a dry cleaner's shop and is a friend of Madame Binet.

Mama hugs us to her and says, "Listen to me, children, this is important. If anyone asks you where your parents are, don't forget that you have to say Papa is a soldier and he's gone to the front. Me, you don't know. Say as little as possible about the things that have happened here in the last little while – the telephones, the radio, the arrests, the informers – not a word! You're Catholic, right, Marguerite? Henriette is responsible for the two of you. She'll be able to explain better." She turns to the woman and says, "Be careful, make sure no one notices you. Are you able to carry their suitcase?"

"I'm small, but I'm agile. Look!" She gets up on the table and then jumps to the ground. After that little demonstration, she says, "Let's get going. I left the downstairs door open. Everything will be fine. Let's go!" She takes charge, just like our maid Georgette... I wonder where she is. I'd rather go away with her, she's twice as big.

I pat Choukette and then I pack my schoolbag. I'm ready, but I'm overcome with sadness. Mama hugs us and kisses us, and then we go outside, where it's still dark. "Goodbye, children! Go, and don't look back. We'll see each other soon," she murmurs, and I hear her blow her nose several times. "Goodbye, Mama," I say, my heart filled with sorrow. The dwarf pulls me behind her.

Part Two:

AT THE MERCY OF OTHERS

The Dry Cleaner's Shop

We spend a week with the dwarf's daughter. She's nice and chats with my sister while she irons the clothes. I listen to the radio and draw at

her desk. We sleep in the attic. I wish I could be with Mama and I miss her almost all the time. We can't stay here because it's too dangerous. Someone will be coming to get us soon.

It's terrible, all the rain we've been having. Luckily, we have our raincoats. The dwarf's daughter gives us the baptismal certificates and we wait for Madame Graziani, who's pretending to be our godmother. That's what I've understood. And what a wonderful surprise it is when she comes! The three of us leave.

Yéyette

The weather is nice but cool. Madame Graziani has us change our coats. She has taken back our baptismal certificates and our textile and food ration cards. We must not lose them. I am terrified and can barely pick up my schoolbag. I walk slowly, hoping at every street corner to see my father and mother. We stop in front of the Denfert-Rochereau métro station, where Madame Graziani's daughter is waiting for us. "Goodbye, Madame Graziani!" We are entrusted to her daughter, whose name is Yéyette. We walk with her for a long time in silence. Will we ever get there?

"Finally, here we are!" declares Yéyette, relieved. It's a convent. "This house is so big, it looks like a prison," says Henriette. I can't stop

shaking. A woman dressed in mourning opens the large door and escorts us to the parlour. She orders us to sit on the bench. Everything feels cold, the people as well as the place. I listen to our story for the second time. I hear Yéyette lying. "I don't know their background. They're orphans." Will they believe it? I'm sobbing against my sister's shoulder and she whispers softly, "Hush, Marguerite." Yéyette kisses us sadly and leaves. Oh, Mama, I'm so afraid.

They give us a little book and the Mother Superior asks us to follow her to the refectory for dinner. Everyone is dressed in black. We'll sleep in a dormitory, separately, each one with her class. They show me my bed, the one against the wall. It's hard and rough. When the others kneel and pray, I remain standing with my head lowered. What am I supposed to do?

"You don't know how to pray?" the girl next to me asks, intrigued.

"I'm not an orphan," I answer in a low voice.

But the lady comes over to me. "I'd like to know why you don't know your prayers?" she asks, helping me climb into my bed to go to sleep. Her hands are clammy. I shake my head. I don't want to speak. She says something to her God. I don't understand nuns. As soon as she goes away, I get my muff out. I burrow into the sheets and, pressing my face into the fur of the muff, I cry my heart out.

Madame Graziani comes to see us. We meet her in the parlour. She gives us some treats – cookies and candies. When the bell rings, she kisses each of us. I finally say what's on my mind, I can't help it. "If you don't take me away from here, I'll yell out that I'm Jewish." Frightened, she puts her hand over my mouth and before leaving says angrily, "Why do you think you're being hidden? Remember, you are CATHOLIC!" I'm upset. And Henriette puts in her two cents. "Now she won't come visit us anymore. Are you happy, baby?"

That night, I wet my bed.

We Leave the Convent

In the late afternoon, someone is to come get us and take us away from here. I'm very glad. I couldn't stay in this convent. When Henriette comes, I tell her, "We're leaving!" with a big smile and she's surprised.

We finally get out of that house. Goodbye, Mother Superior! Goodbye, nuns! Goodbye, my father the priest! I'm so glad to be leaving! A woman I don't know takes me firmly by the hand to cross the street.

At the Gare de Lyon, we get on a train. The woman sits Henriette beside the window because she has motion sickness and puts me in the middle seat so she can keep her eye on me. She sits near us to take care of our papers. At each stop, she's on the lookout. I get up to see what's going on but she makes me go back to my seat. I have to stay seated. I'm responsible for my doll, which is hanging by a rope around my neck, and for my schoolbag. They keep coming to check our papers. But I've found something to distract me – when I went down the aisle, I saw a little boy and he gave me a nice smile. I smile back at him. Now he's playing peek-a-boo with me.

Finally, I feel like I'm going to fall asleep; it's so dark outside. The lady is reading and so is my sister – or else, she's pretending. I stretch out on the seat as if I were with my mother and let the hum of the engine rock me. I feel a delicious warmth. Mama must be at work downstairs in the workshop. Soon she'll be holding me in her arms.

We've arrived! We have to get off. Henriette leans against the window and shouts, "Auntie Sonia!" I'm disappointed, but I still give her a hug. Uncle's car is waiting for us with Riri and Monique playing inside.

There's another surprise! Riri's suitcase is there beside ours, along with a beautiful scooter. But something is not right and that worries me. Auntie isn't answering me the way she usually does. She isn't joking and she won't even look at me. What's going on? We get to a farmhouse and only the adults are asked to come in, while the children are left waiting on the doorstep. I kiss my little cousin Riri. Henriette is playing Mama with baby Monique, who's wriggling – she's so funny!

When the adults come back out, Auntie takes Monique and hurriedly kisses the three of us. Then, without saying a word, the adults put us in a horse-drawn cart, with Henriette and me on one side and the lady and Riri facing us. With alarming speed, they place the suitcases, the three schoolbags, the violin and the scooter in the space in the middle. There isn't time to say goodbye before we're off at a fast clip.

Where are we going? I have no idea. My sister is pouting ... a bad sign. Riri is in the lady's lap, crying. I try to take his hand and give him my doll, but he's inconsolable. The whole way, his distress adds to mine, but I hold back my tears to set an example for him. We'll be together in the same place and I'll take care of him until Auntie comes back. But I'm still troubled.

The Children's Farm

The garden is full of chickens and rabbits. A few children come from different directions to look at the scooter. We go into the house and

the young woman introduces us. "Here are Henriette, Marguerite and their little cousin Riri. You'll see that they're very well brought up and nice. I have to leave now and I'm entrusting them to you." Without any further explanation, she goes away.

We are shown around the farm. We put our things and our cousin's things under the double bed in the corner of the bedroom. Henriette lies down and then I do, and the two of us cry until the sheets are drenched. Riri comes to us and I have to take him in my arms. He doesn't complain. Henriette finally falls into a deep sleep. I think about Mama and I'm angry with her.

Riri is sick. He threw up on the table and he doesn't want to eat. How can we make him feel better? I'm so sad. After a few days, we take him to the bus. Goodbye, Riri! Why are you going away?

The Toilets

The toilets are outside. I go there every morning with Henriette be-cause I'm too small to get up by myself. When she lifts the top, it smells

very bad. There are clouds of flies and mosquitos, and they sting us and buzz around our heads. I need someone to give me a boost up and hold me so that I don't fall down into the hole. I hold my nose the whole time. I can't help getting my bum wet. But there isn't real toilet paper, only newspa-per that hurts and isn't nice.

Henriette Burns Herself

While the farmer's wife irons the clothes, my sister is complaining. I'm under the table listening and not saying anything. "Ow!" cries

Henriette suddenly. The iron has fallen on her hand! Madame Martin empties a bottle of ink on it, but her hand gets more and more swollen, so she rinses it and then puts butter on it instead. My poor sister turns white. "It burns!" she howls in pain. The farmer comes and takes her away in his cart and I watch them disappear down the road.

When they come back in the afternoon, Henriette is half asleep. In the evening, the woman tells us to put our things in our suitcase, reawakening my anxiety about what awaits us. The next day, we're on the road with our bags. I worry all the way. We spent such a short time at this farm, which was so much better than the convent. Poor Henriette! Her hand hurts so much that she's gritting her teeth. But she can't go back to the hospital.

They let us off at the station. The lady who's supposed to take us hasn't arrived yet. Her name is Estelle Évrard. Where will she take us? She arrives just in time to catch the train and she helps me climb up into the car. She says, "We're going to Grenoble. School starts in October and you're lucky, you'll get there at just the right time." I hope my sister gets better quickly. When I see her suffer, it hurts me inside. I cuddle my doll and Henriette strokes her violin case. When we get there, my heart is heavy and my stomach is rumbling.

No, Not in a Convent!

They promised me we wouldn't have to go back there. And now, here they are putting us in another convent! I'll run away. I'll never stay here. If Estelle was nice, she wouldn't leave me with orphans. I don't want to go into this convent. I want to find my mother! I don't have any more tears left to cry and there's nobody to hear me. I don't know how many nights I've slept in the infirmary. They're always watching me. A sister sleeps by my bed, holding her crucifix. There are crucifixes everywhere you look. Every time you turn around, there's another one. The image of Christ on the wall facing me looks as sad as I am. He seems to see me and disapprove. The sister smiles all the time, even when she's sleeping. I pretend to say my prayers but I keep quiet when she comes to listen to me.

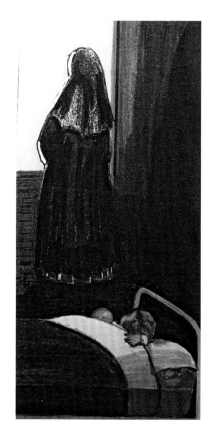

All Alone

This morning when I woke up, I had a premonition of something bad. Last night in the dormitory, the girls were whispering about my doll and the fact that I wouldn't let them play with it. This morning, they laughed at me when I was learning to say, "Hail Mary, full of  grace, the Lord is with thee." While we were praying with our eyes closed, some mysterious thieves ran off with my companion. I've been looking everywhere for her. I know I'll be punished for this. But how will I be able to sleep without her? She is my only friend, the only one I talk to. She sleeps with me. She listens in silence, and even when I don't say anything, she knows what I'm thinking. She's my confessor. I am crying for her.

They're laughing. I woke up with my doll under my arm, but she was half undressed. Where are the clothes Mama knitted for her? They stole them from me. One of the big girls grabs the doll from me and brandishes it like a trophy. She holds it up high so I can't reach it. I jump up, I beg her, but it's no use, she wants me to say my prayer. What does that mean?

"Give it back, or I'll tell! It's mine! It's mine!" I yell so loudly that they hear me on the other side of the partition. The dorm supervisor comes and she's angry. She shouts, "Stop this racket!"

"She started it!" I stammer, in tears. While the girl watches in triumph, the sister grabs my doll and puts it in her cupboard.

Now I'm late, but it doesn't matter. I feel all alone, with only the crucifix for company. Everyone left when the bell rang. What will the teacher say? I dress as quickly as possible. Where are my shoes? The day is starting very badly.

They Make Me Stand in the Corner!

When I walk into the classroom, the teacher leaves for a few minutes. A bunch of mean girls take advantage of her absence to shout insults at me. "Snitch! Tattletale! Crybaby! You'll never get your doll back! They'll confiscate it! You shouldn't have called them!"

I don't know what to do. I'm crying very hard. I'm afraid they won't ever give my doll back. Nobody comes to my defence.

The teacher comes back and calls me up to her desk. She makes me
stand in the corner of the room with my back against the wall until
I calm down. I don't like that woman. She's not fair! I'm the one who
gets in trouble, but I didn't do anything. It's the first time I've had to
stand in the corner and it's just because I wanted to keep my doll. It's
the only thing I have left! I hate you all, every one of you!

I Have Diarrhea

They've put me in a different dormitory. The sister watches me from
the next room. Catholics give me diarrhea, my fear frightens me,
the classes make me freeze, I lie
awake at night. I'm the Little Red
Riding Hood of the school, lost
in a forest surrounded by danc-
ing shadows. I see big bad wolves
under my bed, in the sheets, everywhere. Buried under the covers, I hide my face at the smallest
sound and wait with my heart
pounding. The girls come in
to go to bed. I hear them talking to each other. I get diarrhea
every time I put my fingers in
holy water and make the sign
of the cross. I get diarrhea from
"Our daily bread," from "Our
father who art in heaven." I get
diarrhea from the Good Lord.
Everything's all mixed up in my
head: the "mother," the "sisters,"

the "father-priest" and the Holy Spirit. Almighty God, who sees all
and knows all, has taken my parents away. Nailed to his cross, what

is he doing to help me? I find myself talking to the pretty statue of Mary with her baby in her arms. I like the smell in our house better than that of incense, which irritates my nostrils. I hate the clothes they've given me, they're so itchy! My own clothes are in a storage room under lock and key. I haven't lost my tongue, but every time I say anything, they scold me, so I keep quiet.

I Wash All By Myself

It's hard to wash your back, but I have to. Oh, Papa, if you could see me! If you could hear them! I'm not "dirty"! But when we wash, I can't stand them touching me.

The sister berates me, "Scrub! Scrub harder, you won't wear away your body. Don't forget the little corners." I scrub myself so well and so hard that I scratch my skin with their abrasive glove. She looks behind our ears, around our necks, between our fingers and even between our toes and our thighs. I stand there naked, silent, shivering.

This Sunday morning, after the medical examination, they cut my nails very short. I don't like it. "Where does this blood come from, wretched girl?" asks the sister, looking for bugs in my hair because I scratch myself a lot. "Good Lord! You're crawling with lice!" she ex-

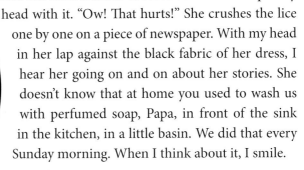

claims. She takes her fine-toothed comb and scrapes my head with it. "Ow! That hurts!" She crushes the lice one by one on a piece of newspaper. With my head in her lap against the black fabric of her dress, I hear her going on and on about her stories. She doesn't know that at home you used to wash us with perfumed soap, Papa, in front of the sink in the kitchen, in a little basin. We did that every Sunday morning. When I think about it, I smile.

The Merry-Go-Round

I take off the convent rags I wear every day and put on my Sunday clothes. No more penance! I'm going to show off my beautiful dress, my coat of white rabbit fur, my hat and my gloves to the city of Grenoble! The bell rings. We're going out! Last night during prayers, I didn't pretend. I spoke to my father and since then, I've been filled with hope. I was even able to sleep again.

In the street, two by two in a long line, we follow the Mother Superior without making any noise. She is way ahead of us. In the silence of the deserted street, I hear the music of a barrel organ. I let it waltz into my head and my heart – it's a Parisian song. Then, at the corner where the street meets a boulevard, I see the merry-go-round. All our eyes are riveted to it. The wooden horses, the music, the lights and the rounded roof that protects it from the rain are just like the one in Place Voltaire, where the children would line up and wait, holding their tickets and laughing with excitement. And I did too, right in front of the Germans. When I go back to the Luxembourg Gardens, I'll be big enough to get up on the horse by myself and maybe I'll even choose my horse before Henriette does. My parents will be there hand in hand. They'll pop out and surprise us and we'll sing to the music of a brass band in the middle of the park. Then we'll watch the puppet show and laugh ourselves silly and have a cup of hot chocolate.

A hand grabs me. "Where are you going, child?" Without noticing, I've gone ahead of the Mother Superior. I store my precious dream carefully in my memory.

It Wasn't Me!

I feel a gentle, rolling motion. I'm floating, carried by the waves, like a fish in a net. No, I'm not floating, someone is holding me and handling me. I feel someone putting pants on me. I hear someone whisper, "Quick, she's waking up!" Then I hear steps moving away. I'm shivering. This is not a nightmare, I'm lying in my bed in the dormi-

tory and I'm awake. I squint, but all I can see are shadows in the darkness. A bad smell is coming from my bedclothes and I feel something cold and wet on my bum. The dorm supervisor turns the light on. She's making her round as usual. I sit up and sneeze. "Atchoo!" She stops beside me. "Atchoo!" I sneeze again, in spite of myself.

She sniffs, and then she slaps me, saying, "So it's you making that awful smell!"

"I guess so," I admit in a small voice, shocked at being slapped. I feel mocking looks all around me. My sheets are befouled with something brown and there's an unmistakeable smell of poop. The sister takes off my pyjama bottoms, exposing the evidence of my disgrace dripping down my shaking legs. It's revolting! She picks them up with the tips of her fingers and holds them up so everyone can see them. All the girls laugh. I'm crying so hard I can't even breathe. My face is red and I'm filled with shame.

"Go to the sink, young lady!" she orders. "I'll join you there."

I go to wash and realize that someone has played a dirty trick on me – my underpants are still on and they're clean inside! "It wasn't me, sister!" But the sister has gone and I can't find her.

Arrival at the Chatenays'

With intense excitement, I put on my Sunday clothes. I take all my things and go the the Mother Superior's office. What a joy to find my sister there! She's sitting on the bench with her schoolbag at her feet and her violin case on her lap, and her cheeks are pink. "We're going to the country, to the village of Vatilieu, in a valley in the middle of the mountains," she whispers in my ear. Here we go again. I don't like all these sudden departures and trips with strangers. I thought that was over, but apparently it isn't.

Earlier, when they gave me back my doll, ev-  erything suddenly seemed better. They told me I would be getting good news and I was so happy I was walking on air. But now I'm filled with apprehension.

A lady comes to get us, as usual. This one is called Colette Morel. She carries our suitcase.

Who will I be with tomorrow? "Quickly, young ladies, we have to take the train," she announces cheerfully. I've taken it so many times that it doesn't have any effect on me. This is all supposed to be for our own good. Henriette reads a magazine with lots of pictures. I watch the countryside go by.

We finally get off and then walk for a long time, a very long time. I have to keep changing my schoolbag from one hand to the other. A bell rings. In the building opposite us, boys and girls come out, jostling each other. That must be the teacher standing at the door. Maybe she's waiting for us. We stay there for a moment and then go on.

A little bit further and we're there. "Here's your new home," says Colette Morel. My head is itching. I see cows and horses. I can smell manure from the stable. We are introduced to the farmers, the Chatenays. Our guide is in a hurry. She hands them our suitcase, says goodbye to us and leaves.

The man, Robert, smiles and jokes and seems very jolly. The grandmother knitting in a corner is his Mama. There's another woman, Antoinette, who's the lady of the house. She seems more severe than her husband and she's also taller. She gives the orders: "Come here!" "Put that there!" "Do this!" "Do that!"

After a delicious snack – I still have my eye on the cake that's left – she shows us around. They have a grocery store. I see blocks of butter, cream cheese, barrels of wine, and several kinds of bread and milk. I won't die of hunger.

We go upstairs and Madame Chatenay shows us our room. My sister and I will sleep together in the double bed, under the crucifix on the wall. "Careful not to dirty my bedspread," she says with a scowl, noticing traces of earth.

We scratch ourselves constantly. "Get your clothes off now! You need a good shower." She pushes us toward the bathroom and gathers up our clothes, examines them and takes them away, as they did at the convent. To make sure we're clean, she scrubs us all over. Then she dries us. Then she picks up a brush and starts to do our hair. "Holy Mary, mother of Jesus! You're full of lice! We'll have to get rid of those dirty bugs!" she exclaims, throwing each of us a towel.

We go downstairs and she leads us outside. She brings out two chairs from the kitchen, a big basin and a pitcher of hot water. She shampoos Henriette's hair first. Without worrying about the neighbours who are watching, she soaps her hair. If only I could stick my tongue out at them! She rinses Henriette's hair and pours a bottle of gasoline on it. "Ow, it burns!" yells my poor sister, who seems to have it in her ears. The lady wraps her head in the towel and sits her down. Then, pointing a finger at me, she says, "Now it's your turn."

Ah! So You Like Milk!

"Since you like milk so much, do you know where it comes from?"
Monsieur Chatenay asks me. "Of course I know – it comes from
cows!" I answer immediately. Surprised by my knowledge, he asks
me to follow him to the stable. He slaps the back of the nearest cow
and rubs her udder. "Well, I'll show you how to milk a cow!" He sits
down on a small stool. I stay a little distance away; I don't want to get
hit by a foot or a tail.

He grasps the tubes of pink flesh with his hands and pulls them
up and down. It doesn't seem to hurt the cow. White liquid flows into
the bucket slowly and then in gushes. Then he turns his head toward

me, teasing me the way you hold out a carrot to a rabbit. "Come here,
pet! She won't eat you. These big animals are herbivorous. They don't
eat meat. Okay, missy, open your mouth. I'll give you a taste, nice and
warm, straight from this one's udder!"

I stand there with my legs apart, firmly grounded. I don't say anything, I just open my mouth wide in a big laugh. And he makes the
milk spurt right into my mouth! It's not bad, but I like it better cold.
I'm so delighted by this feat that I run and tell Henriette about it, but

she won't listen because it makes her sick. Now, whenever I drink milk, I think about my special feat.

I Don't Like the Skin on Milk

Trying to avoid the watchful eyes of the farmer's wife, I remove the skin from the milk in my bowl of coffee. "You little fool!" she exclaims. "What are you doing? You're throwing away the best part!"

"I can't swallow it, it sticks in my throat. It makes me feel like throwing up."

My sister bursts out laughing. Madame Chatenay opens a drawer and takes out an old strainer. She gives it to me with another bowl, saying, "Pour the milk through it and stop making those faces!" I obey and then I drink my milk in one gulp.

"I'd rather have butter, please," I say, scraping my knife on my bread. The farmer's wife takes my hand and bellows, "You don't like my jam? It's war jam, made with peels and seeds. Don't you like it?"

"No, I don't like the seeds. They hurt when I swallow."

"It's wrong to waste food. You must have been really spoiled! We don't waste anything here. Remember that, young lady!"

The Doctor

He is finally here! "We've been waiting for you for hours," says Madame Chatenay with a sigh when she opens the door for the doc-

tor. Henriette is very sick. She threw up her whole meal. She's burning up and has a fever over 40°C. Madame Chatenay gives her water on a spoon. My sister keeps calling for Mama. What's serious is that in her delirium, she speaks of our parents. I hope the Chatenays haven't heard her. I'm terribly afraid. I don't want her to die. Even if she annoys me! Please, God, I beg you, let her live. The doctor comes downstairs looking very worried. It's my turn to be examined. The adults are talking among themselves.

The doctor sits down in the kitchen to write a prescription. I'm imagining horrible things. I approach him timidly and ask, "She won't die, will she?"

"No, I don't think so."

Then I show him my doll, whose head is coming off. He listens to her heart with his stethoscope. He asks me the same questions again. If he keeps this up, I'll collapse. I also have a fever.

"What did your parents do in Paris?"

"I don't know," I stammer.

He takes me by the hand and we go up to the bedroom next to ours, the grandmother's bedroom. He starts asking me questions again. "Have you had measles? Whooping cough? Chicken pox?"

"Only measles. When I was with my mother."

"Are these fur coats yours? They're very beautiful."

"My Papa made them!" I say proudly and immediately regret it. He spreads out a towel and places his head gently against my chest, then looks at my neck and feels it all over. It seems I have a goiter.

After we say goodbye to the doctor, I notice that Robert Chatenay has repaired my doll. He hands  her to me, saying, "Now that she's better, we'll take care of you two. We'll do cupping."

"What's cupping?"

"Here are the cups. There are nine of them."

They look like yogurt jars.

Henriette is still sleeping. I'm lucky they're going to start with her. I'm drenched in perspiration. Using a cotton pad dipped in alcohol, they create a vacuum inside each cup with the flame of a candle. Then they turn the cup upside down on her back, as if they were building a sand castle at the beach. From time to time, my sister cries out, "Mama! Mama!" as if our mother could hear her. Now they've placed the last cup on her back. After that, it will be my turn. I'm trembling with fear.

The Raspberries Near the Toilet

The bushes are full of raspberries just waiting to be tasted. They make your mouth water, but they prick your fingers. They're so beautiful they call out to me, "Don't wait for us to rot, pick us now." So, too bad

if it's a sin, I give in to temptation. They're so delicious! Hurry now, have you forgotten that they're waiting for you? If you're in the toilet too long, you'll get in trouble.

What a surprise at supper when, for dessert, there's a big bowl full of – guess what? Oh, horror! A mountain of raspberries! My face feels hot; I must be as red as the berries. I'm soaked with sweat. God is punishing me! "Taste them, pet! Take as many as you want!"

Antoinette Chatenay says. And I feel really silly. She presents the little berries, admiring and savouring them.

In the bedroom when it's time to go to sleep, I have a guilty conscience and my stomach is upset. What had been so sweet has become bitter.

My Tooth Is Hanging by a Thread

For a week, my tooth has been bothering me. I try not to think about it, but I can't help playing with it with my tongue. Monsieur Chatenay asks me, "Do you want me to pull it out for you? It's hanging by a thread." Who does he think he is? He's not my father. And he's not a dentist. I say no. My sister looks at me mockingly. "You're such a chicken!" Robert leaves the table, saying, "I have a great remedy. You'll see. You'll like it."

I grip the chair. He opens a kitchen drawer, takes out a spool of white string and ties the end of the string to the doorknob of the opened front door. He walks slowly toward me, letting the string out as he goes. Then he cuts the string and ties the other end around my tooth. Finally, he says, "Okay, I'm going now." And he slams the door behind him as he goes. My tooth flies right out of my mouth! I didn't even have time to say ouch, it was already gone. Now he's waiting for me to thank him. I approach him timidly, get up on his knee, and kiss him on the cheek. We both smile. This is my way of saying thank you to him.

The Chatenay family, summer 1943.

It's Not Fair!

No! I didn't wipe my fingers on the wall! It's not true, it wasn't me, I swear. They're the ones who are lying, both Granny and my sister. And they dare to tell me it's wrong to lie. I'm the small-est, so they blame everything on me! As punish-ment, I have to clean the wall. If only Georgette were here, she would clean it for me. But there's no one to defend me. I can shout all I want, no-body will hear me. The Chatenays have locked the door and gone to mass to hear the priest preach. The Good Lord, who is everywhere, who sees all and knows all, will not forgive them for this. I can  shout the truth all I want but nobody listens to me. I'm too young to do housecleaning. It's not fair! And after what they've done, they want me to like them. They'll wait a long time, a very long time. I'll tell my parents. Oh, Mama, I'm weeping in despair.

The Heating Brick

On cold winter nights, after supper has been cooked and we're setting the table, Granny puts some bricks in the oven. When it's time to go up to bed, Madame Chatenay spreads towels on the table. Using her big tongs, she takes the bricks out of the oven one by one and puts each one of them in the middle of one of the white towels, taking care not to burn her hands. Then she wraps each one up just like

Auntie Sonia used to do when she wrapped my little cousin Monique in swaddling. And as usual, she chooses my sister. "Here, child, take this to your room and put it right in the middle of the bed." I haven't told her
that Henriette doesn't obey – she puts the brick on her side of the bed. Because when I look at the bars at the head of the bed and count them out loud, I see that there are three bars on my sister's side and four bars on mine. She always has the last word.

I have to fight with my big sister. Every night, it's the same story. The one who lies down first gets to put her feet on the brick. She's the one who wins, again. Of course. I always lose. Buried under the blankets, cursing her, I close my eyes, but I imagine her triumphant smile. Despite her sin of selfishness, she falls asleep. That's when I move the brick to my side of the bed to warm up my cold feet.

My Wicker Basket

Robert is making me a wicker basket. He's in the barn, where I watch him weave. I know better than to interrupt him. I sing songs from school for him. He knows more of them than I do and from time to time, he sings with me. He knows how to work the branches, over, under, over, under, making sure there are no holes and curving them to form a handle. "This is for you, child, so I want to do it right," he says, without lifting his head. In silence, I admire his work.

But after a little while, he's no longer the one I'm watching. In my thoughts, I picture Mama in her workshop. I worry that this image of her will fade from my memory: I am sitting at the bottom of the stairs waiting impatiently and I ask her, "How much longer are you going to be?" Sometimes, she'd ask me to try clothes on and I'd strut around in front of her, imitating her customers. And when the clothes fit well, she'd smile at me and I'd be so happy.

Robert is nice to me, but he isn't my Papa. He's so different. Papa would play like a child. Once, he put me in my doll's carriage and pushed it, running really fast. The carriage broke and my feet hit the pavement. We laughed our heads off. If I was unhappy, he would pick me up and cuddle me. Life was a lot more fun than it is here. I remember the way he smelled, a sweet smell of flowers.

This basket will be my Christmas present and the first gift that I'll be able to keep. It will be placed in my clogs that I put in front of the fireplace. When I wish the Chatenays a happy New Year, I'll save a few good wishes for my real parents.

The Second Christmas at Vatilieu

It's very cold out, but in the house the wood stove envelops my body in its warmth. I set the table in silence, on the beautiful white table-

Photograph, torn but full of life, of my first birthday party, at our house. I am surrounded by my family. December 1936. From left to right: my aunt Sara (murdered in Treblinka); my uncle Léon (made prisoner and survived the war); his wife, my aunt Rose; my father and mother with us on their laps; Salomon, known as "Poupko," an admirer of my auntie Sonia; Aunt Sonia; and her husband, Uncle Wolf, who was so nice.

cloth. The aromas from the kitchen fill the whole house. I savour the raspberry pie in anticipation.

Immersed in the happy sweetness, I suddenly go back in my imagination and see myself with my mother at one of our meals on special days.

I remember Saturday evening meals, when my father would turn off the lights, light candles and say to everyone, "Bon appétit!" You could see the joy in our eyes and on our faces in the candlelight that danced to the rhythm of

the music playing on the radio. What beauty! Everything was so good: chicken soup with *knaidlach* – matzah balls – and the neck stuffed with onions cooked in goose fat – *gribenes*. There were also latkes, delicious pan-fried potato pancakes. For dessert, we had my favourite Franco-Russe chocolate pudding, which I would eat very slowly. I'd enjoy my meal under the protective gaze of my parents – where are they now?

Here, I get potatoes au gratin made especially for me and to end the meal, a delectable dessert that I love. But I am desperately unhappy. "On Christmas Eve," says the priest, "Jesus Christ was born in Bethlehem." I was born in Paris in the 19th arrondissement. And I feel totally alone.

I'm sad because in the big nativity scene at the church, I saw baby Jesus surrounded by his family. My family was taken from me and nobody says anything about it. In my bed after midnight mass, I smother my tears and hold my doll in my arms. In spite of my pain, I fall asleep in Papa's arms, the only place where I feel I truly belong.

The Logs and the Hoop

Granny Chatenay had to take down the hems of our fur coats. It seems we're the only girls around here who have such nice coats. There are lots of rabbits, but few good furriers. *They* were in Paris, now *they* are gone and *he* was sent to Drancy.

Nobody really bothers me – except my sister, of course. When she bosses me around, I stand up to her, but I don't answer back as much. No fighting, no scolding. So I mostly keep my mouth shut. I open it every once in a while to show that I still have a good sharp tongue.

This is my second winter in Vatilieu. Things have been going better lately. We're the Chatenays' girls, the children of the Holy Family! Yes, I leave food at meals. I give my fat to the dog, who really likes it. But he makes so much noise that I get scolded. "There are orphans who are much worse off than you. They are dying of hunger because there is a war on and they have no money and live in misery. And you, you're so fussy!" Who are they saying this to? They're forgetting all the children who are with their real parents. Where are mine? I don't know. Save your sermons for bad people and for the *Boches*!

When they criticize me, I'd rather go outside and breathe freely than answer with insults. I fly far away in the sky, beyond the farm,

to the Luxembourg Gardens. I'll go back there someday. I'll be wearing a new dress that Mama will knit for me. And I'll have shining ringlets that she'll make by rolling my hair around her fingers. I can see her making them and tying them with a bow.

I'm running after my hoop the way I used to do, under a radiant sky. I hear Papa behind me saying, "Stop! Stop!" I'm going too fast now, he can't catch me. I'm over eight now. I see my parents standing on the steps, tenderly holding each other. I look at them longingly.

Suddenly: "Mar-gue-rite!" It's Robert Chatenay. He sounds angry. I was forgetting the logs I was supposed to bring back. "Come on, child! We're ready to light the fire in the fireplace, we're just waiting for you. Hurry up!" Oh, if only I could just lose myself in my dreams.

Glasses Just Like Papa's

For a long time, I've been complaining of difficulty when reading from a distance. I had even been punished by having to stand in the corner at school. Finally, they took me far from Vatilieu to have my eyes examined and could see that I was telling the truth. It appears that I'm

nearsighted. It's hereditary. But it doesn't matter because I'm like my father. I'm so happy, I can't keep from laughing.

"We're going to get glasses," Antoinette Chatenay shouts to Granny, who's dozing.

"What is it you want now, little birdbrain?" asks Robert, tapping me gently on the head.

"If we're going to the doctor's, I want to show him my doll. Her arms are falling off again."

"What a little character you are! Go on, go get it, but hurry up. Toinette is waiting for you there."

We climb into the cart at the door to the school and I sit with my back against the side. Giddy-up, and the horses pull the cart. To pass the time, I go to sleep, or rather, pretend to sleep.

They sometimes forget that my name is Marguerite. I don't always deserve the names they call me – "birdbrain," "difficult," "spoiled,"

"silly." How can I make them stop saying these things without getting sent to a convent? Where are my parents? I've been waiting for them for an eternity. Are they dead? Are they still alive? The war goes on and on. It will never end! We'll stay with the Chatenays and become farmers like them. Henriette wants to receive her first communion in a white bridal dress. When we change the sheets on the bed, she dresses up in them. And I can't say anything to her because my opinion doesn't count; she thinks everything I say is stupid. If they keep mixing up my brain, I won't know what my name is.

The optician adjusts my glasses. "They're ready now. They're yours. Look at yourself in the mirror." Perched on the stool, I wait for the case to put my glasses in when I'm not wearing them. I squint

and knit my brow the way Papa used to do, and I see his gentle face opposite me, looking at me. Yes, I look more like him now. We smile at each other in silence, looking at each other tenderly.

"So, Marguerite. Are you happy?" The image disappears like a shooting star. "Aren't you going to say thank you?" Madame Chatenay asks, helping me get down. I don't want to listen to her. She shakes my arm, repeating, "What do we say?"

"Thank you. Thank you very much." I say obediently, forcing myself to be polite. On the way home, I search for my father in the clouds. I play with my glasses, raising and lowering them on my nose. It's strange, everything looks clearer, the Isère region and Vatilieu.

As soon as I'm alone in the bedroom with no one around, I go to the mirror. I admire myself full face and in profile, with different

expressions. Then I close my eyes and imagine that my father is kissing my eyelids,
and I sit down. He's in his armchair in
front of me, showing me how to count
on my fingers, the way he did when I
turned five and he took me in his lap
and gave me that number of kisses on
the cheeks, plus one for the next day.
Today, my two hands are not enough
for me to count to a thousand. And
there's no point.

Ski for Two

Leaving the church, "Mama" gives me a kiss in front of the parish-
ioners. I don't know why, but my immediate reaction is to hate it.
I really hope that during confession the priest doesn't try to get the

truth out of me. As long as I go to confession, the
priest doesn't harrass me. He doesn't tolerate being lied to. So if he asks, should I say that she's not
my mother? Just because I call her "Mama" from
time to time doesn't mean I belong to her. It's ir-
ritating. Just this morning at the table, she asked
us, "Was breakfast good? Are you finished? Can I
clear the table?" To avoid her cloying concern, I look up at the ceiling.
My sister washes the dishes and I dry them.

"Papa" also has some charming things to say. "Aren't you finished
yet, sweethearts? I was hoping you'd be ready." Why is he saying this
to us? And he starts in again with "Look how splendid the weather is
today! It's a perfect day to do what I've been planning. We're going to
go skiing two by two, the whole family together." He's really laying it
on. What is he thinking? No, really, it rings false in my ears.

The Chatenays have a loud discussion: she says we should take the sled and he says we should take skis. She says skiing is a sport for adults. I've put my glasses away so that they won't get broken. We leave Granny with her knitting and the dog to guard the house. We put on our rabbitskin coats. Once we're outside, I breathe in the sweetness of my eighth spring. The sled is in the barn and my sister pokes me with her elbow so that I'll go get it.

"Come on, we'll take you! You'll like it, you'll see. Skiing is amazing! Incredible! Unimaginable! Incomparable!" Robert says. In his monologue, our joker forgot "Horrible!" and "Dreadful!" I'm sulking. I don't feel like going skiing.

"All aboard, gang!" Robert cries cheerfully. Stubborn as a mule, I drag my feet on purpose to make everyone slow down. I don't want to go skiing. I would much rather  go sledding. I know that when I go sledding with Henriette, I sometimes complain because my sister pushes me and makes me fall head first into the snow. But it's not that I dislike going sledding. Quite the contrary – I just want to be the one to steer. It's natural that I rebel and that we argue. But I'm the one they scold and not the older one. That hurts. Adults think I'm a whiner, but they don't know that I love to lie down in the powdery snow when I'm all bundled up. With my eyes closed, my arms and legs stretched out to the four points of the compass, I pretend I'm going to sleep in a huge, immaculate white bed under the shining golden rays of the sun.

At the edge of the ski trail, the Chatenays separate us. "The older one with mother, the little one with father." I'm still frightened by the silence of the cemetery we've just passed without anyone seeming to notice. Robert laces up his leather boots and gives me a smile and wink. Then he stands up and dashes forward, shouting, "Look at me! Next time, you'll come with me!" What does he think – that I'm going to follow him? At the same time, I see my sister plastered against

Toinette, standing on her skis. They go hurtling down the mountain stuck together like that. Then they both fall, yelling their heads off. "S.O.S! Every man for himself!" Dear God! When Robert comes back, will I have to go down the hill like that too? I don't want to hold on to his backside in this manner; it's disgusting.

Maybe I can get out of it if I pray. I close my eyes. "In the name of the Father, the Son and the Holy Ghost. Amen. I beseech you to take me a thousand miles away from here!" Has God heard me?

Am I seeing things? Is that me astride Papa's back, with him on all fours on the green carpet in the living room? Giddy-up! Giddy-up!

 I hang on with every leap so as not to fall off. Like the rider in the circus, I spur him on. Then I hug him. My cheek against his, I say quietly, "Oh, I love you!" When he stands up, I'm hanging on his neck and he walks around, whistling one of his favourite songs.

"Une fleur au chapeau, à la bouche un vieux mégot…" That's not my father's song! It's Robert who's humming this one! Alas, the man standing in front of me is not my father. Robert gets impatient and comes over to me. The comforting image of my real father has confused me. "Tell me, Marguerite, you wouldn't by any chance be scared, would you?" He's teasing me, but I don't react. "Come on! Get on my skis and you'll see. They go down all by themselves. Hold on tight to my legs. Okay? Here we go!"

He puts me on and down we go, heading straight for disaster. I hold on tight to him and we plunge into the void. It's too fast! I'm so small, I've got my face up against his bum. It makes me uncomfortable but I don't say anything. We go head over heels and everything's upside down. Mama! Mama! We've fallen in the snow!

"Not too bad for the first time. You see, you can do it!" the expert says, chuckling. I climb back up the hill, discouraged. But my mood begins to improve because the second time is much better. And the third time, I'm actually enjoying myself. The fourth time, my fear is completely gone. And the fifth time, thank you, God! Robert is persistent and unlike my sister he never gets mad at me. I am very proud of myself!

Auntie Sonia

The teacher takes me out of the class, saying it's urgent. My heart is beating very hard. My sister is ahead of me. When we get home,

Madame Chatenay says, without looking us in the eye, "Put on your Sunday dresses. We're going to Grenoble, someone is waiting for us there." What's happening? The Chatenays don't look pleased. Could it be that the concierge, that gossip, has informed on us again? "Trash!" That was the last name Mama called her and she was right.

"Don't bother bringing your doll. It's just a visit," Monsieur Chatenay whispers, taking my doll from me. He's dressed up and I wonder why. He puts her on the sideboard, saying, "It will be fine here. Nobody will take it from you."

"Yes, but what if I – " I stammer nervously, my heart pounding. I'm afraid I'm being tricked. I don't want to listen to him. I should bring

her with me. They know she was confiscated at the convent. I've told them so many times.

Our cart stops in front of Notre-Dame-de-Sion. My teeth are chattering. The name alone brings back bad memories. Are they going to punish me again? Darkness, cold, all my worst fears come back to me. I mustn't cry, but how can I calm my apprehension? We ring at the main door and our escorts abandon us, saying, "We'll see you later!" Really?

Henriette is as silent as a stone. She looks around nervously at the austere surroundings. The doorknob moves. My face is on fire, I must be scarlet. I breathe as deeply as I can and then Henriette and I say in unison to the women who've opened the door to us, "Good day, sister. Good day, Mother."

They stare at us. "Don't they look like good little girls!" And the Mother Superior holds out her hands to us and guides us to the waiting room. An elegant woman is dozing in an armchair, almost falling out of the chair. But when she sees us, she starts.

"Auntie Sonia?" exclaims Henriette, who has recognized her before I did. "Auntie Sonia?"

"Finally," she sighs, getting up suddenly. "My dear little girls! Tell me it's really you!"

"You shouldn't have come, Auntie! They'll know – " says Henriette.

"Shh!" Auntie interrupts, putting her hand over Henriette's mouth, "Don't vorry. That's vy I'm vearing this veil!" she says with the accent I suddenly remember. She lifts the veil and I approach her. I recognize the beautiful face of my aunt beneath the hat. "Auntie Sonia!" I'm so delighted to see her!

She looks at us tenderly and explains, "I vanted to be sure you vere alive. I'm so happy to see you, I can hardly believe it." She takes out a handkerchief and dabs at the makeup on her eyes. Then she blows her nose hard. I want to kiss her, but when will I be able to? She takes the big one in her arms and they have a whispered conversation, but I'm still waiting.

Finally, Auntie turns toward me. "Hello, baby, how are you? Vat's happened to your chubby cheeks?"

"Everyone here calls me Marguerite," I say quickly.

"So, Marguerite, aren't you eating enough? Don't you get any treats? I'm bringing you some sveets." She says *v* instead of *w*. "Don't eat more than one a day, my sveethearts, promise?" The sister smiles slyly.

"Promise," we answer together.

Auntie holds us to her and kisses each of us on our forehead, our chin and even our neck. We talk a lot.

"It's time for your train, Madame," the sister says gravely. The church bells ring four o'clock, reverberating in my soul and spoiling my pleasure.

"Already? My goodness! Thank you, sister, thank you for everything. Excuse me for troubling you. I had no choice. I'm sure you understand."

I doubt that she understands. But the Mother Superior nods her head. "Of course I understand. May God be the witness to my compassion for you."

Auntie puts her coat on and kisses us again. Then she leaves reluctantly, saying, "Goodbye, children. May God protect us all." I'm shaking all over. Her voice is so soft.

"Goodbye, Auntie! Thank you for the parcel," we answer.

Back at home, I inhale her perfume on the back of my hand. I go to bed holding my doll and transfer the wonderful smell to her. I feel sad. Lost in my thoughts, I'm unable to fall asleep.

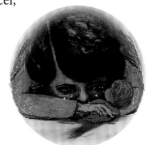

My Good Fauvette

Luckily I have you. Nobody else listens to me. It is the school fête. There's a party at school for everyone – everyone but me. I knew my song perfectly and I had rehearsed it out loud without a mistake. "They're the girls from La Rochelle...." And they took it away from me. I'm not talking to them anymore, those cows! Oh, sorry, I don't mean you. You're my favourite cow. You're the gentlest one. I can tell you anything. We understand each other. They're all thieves, even my own sister. Someone stole her song, Schubert's "The Trout":

Across a clear brook gentle,
There shot in eager haste

The trout, so temperamental;
Quite arrow-like it raced.

So she went ahead and stole mine. Why did she have to take my song? She knows dozens of them. "The Linden Trees," for example:

This is the peaceful spot
When the sun goes down
Where I love to come and sit
Far from the noise of the town.

No, she has no consideration. Instead of that, she sang "The Girls From La Rochelle." It will bring her bad luck, you'll see. I'm still upset over it. I didn't want to, but I was forced to make do with "Madame Bread-and-Butter," about a lady who lives in a candy house. I stuttered and stammered my way through it and it was no picnic, I can tell you. The audience shouted, "Madame Bread-and-Butter! Give it to us!" You should have seen my face. Instead of applauding, they laughed and sang "Don't cry, Jeannette!" They're beasts, Fauvette, not like you. Luckily, I have you.

Mardi Gras

The whole village is in a festive mood. All the children our age are wearing costumes and going from house to house eating crêpes. Cécile and Denise, Antoinette's nieces, have dressed us up in their clothes, which are a bit too long for us. They've made us paper masks that tie with strings at the backs of our heads. Henriette is showing off in her high heels, but she's having trouble walk-
ing. I'd rather have the cap Robert has loaned me – at least there's no danger that I'll twist my ankle.

The old gentleman across the way offers us French fries. He puts them right in our mouths and we really eat a lot. The paper of our masks soaks up the grease and they tear. We laugh ourselves silly. He  cuts out new masks and puts them on our faces. We look at ourselves in the mirror. They don't look too bad.

My sister walks carefully, swaying from one foot to the other. To avoid stumbling, I do the same. People are very welcoming to us everywhere we go. After an hour, we're full. Since we've had enough crêpes, Madame Chatenay puts away the ones she's made for later.

On the Hill of the Birds

You get out of breath climbing the hill to Madame Chatenay's cousin's house, but there's such a beautiful view from up there. While Antoinette is chatting in the big house, where she has spread out the things she's brought, we go out to the fountain with the birds. I tear little bits off my slice of bread and jam and throw them to the pigeons, who peck hungrily at them and coo. I call to them, "Here birdie, birdie, birdie!"

"When are you going to shut up?" my bossy sister asks. I shrug; she's being her usual, controlling self. I keep calling, "Here birdie, birdie, birdie!" No one can say I'm wasting food. I'm feeding the family that André, Antoinette's nephew, has tamed. Henriette thinks she's so interesting with her bird on her arm. She's lucky I'm not mean. I look the other way and, to annoy her, I sing:

> There once was a little man
> Named Guillery Carabi.
> A-hunting he did go
> For a pheasant, or two or three
> Carabi titi, carabi toto, carabo...

"Can't you shut up?" my sister repeats irritably. She doesn't scare me. The bird warbles to encourage me and mock her. Henriette gives me a kick that makes me fall into the water.

"That's not funny! My dress is all wet now because of you. If Mama sees it, I'll get scolded."

"You asked for it!"

"That's not true! You pushed me."

"You're crazy! You're making a big fuss about nothing. And because of you, my bird flew away. I'll make you shut up!"

Madame Chatenay appears on the doorstep. We stop fighting immediately. I am relieved because that squabble could have turned nasty and we would have been scolded. She asks, "Are you being good, girls? My cousin is offering you a drink." I don't dare sit down and I'm dripping on the kitchen floor. I take my glass of milk and go back to my feathered friend while the other birds nibble.

À la claire fontaine,
M'en allant promener,
J'ai trouvé l'eau si belle,
Que je m'y suis baignée.
Il y a longtemps que je t'aime,
Jamais je ne t'oublierai....

At the clear spring
I stopped along my way.
The water was so lovely
I stayed there to bathe.
I've loved you for a long time.
Never will I forget you....

This song is painful and joyful at the same time. The bird flaps its wings and flies away toward another one. A feather floats down and I catch it and hold it in my hand.

We Kill the Pig

Early one morning, our sidewalk becomes an abattoir. We're going to kill a pig. The Chatenays have chosen the fattest sow. She fed her children when they were small and her work is done. The whole house is busy preparing – even Granny has put down her knitting for the occasion. Some men have come to help. They place a board on trestles and put a stepladder behind it. Then they sharpen the knives. In the kitchen, everyone is in a good mood while we polish the pots. We spread white sheets on the tables. Everything has to be absolutely spotless. We pile up the pots and pans, bowls and basins. There's no space left in the kitchen. Everything is ready for the butchering.

The executioners have a jolly look. When they bring the sow out of the pigsty, I pity the poor animal. She must sense that she's going to die because she doesn't want to come. Luckily, I'm watching from inside the house, through the window. But the door is open. Several of the men are holding her. I feel for her suffering and I'm a little afraid. The butcher sticks the shining blade of his knife into the neck of the howling animal and slits her throat. It's horrible! The blood spurts out into a basin. Antoinette brings the basin and puts it down in front of me. I act as if I don't see it, but I feel like vomiting.

"Feel it, it's still warm," she says, and then, looking at me, "You're a bit pale. Go outside." I go out reluctantly. I'll never eat ham or black pudding again; they've spoiled them for me.

They've hung the sow by its back feet from the top of the stepladder. I think of its piglets. Surrounded by his friends, Robert proudly holds up the dripping head for the indispensable photograph. The carcass hangs, its belly empty. With morbid curiosity, I watch them cutting off pieces and preparing the hams. They wash the entrails to fill them with sausage meat. Granny boils the blood for the black pudding. We salt the rest and pack it in a box called a salting box. We won't run short of meat this winter.

Their work done, the men celebrate with glasses of white wine and sing drinking songs: "Ah, le petit vin blanc " (Ah, a nice glass of white wine), "Boire un petit coup c'est agréable" (Drinking wine feels so good), and the most appropriate one, "J'aime le jambon et la saucisse, mais j'aime encore mieux le lait de ma nourrice" (I like ham and sausage, but what I like best is my nursemaid's milk).

A Strange Meeting

We've been discussing it for an hour. My sister is looking for an argument. I walk away, feigning a stomachache. I walk to the toilet as if to go in, but I don't. I go down the stairs on tiptoe, without making any noise, and head toward the stable. The dark doesn't scare me, I know the whole house from the attic to the basement. I open the barn door and a light blinds me. Strange, in the middle of the night.

Crouching on the edge of the loft, like a watchdog ready to attack, there's a young man with his eyes riveted on me. Where did he come

from? What is he doing here in pyjamas? With me watching inquisitively, he stretches and yawns deeply. Then he grabs the railing and stands up, still staring at me. My goodness, he's tall! I'm not afraid of him because he has a nice face. The bawling of one of the animals in the stable shatters the silence. We smile at each other, thanking the stars that have brought us together.

Without a word, I walk out, lifting the hem of my nightgown so that it doesn't get dirty. I don't say anything to anyone. I take off my shoes, go upstairs and stand in the doorway of my room. My sister is snoring on her pillow.

She's wearing her rosary as if it were a necklace. She's a real Catholic! Lying in my half of the bed, I think about the stranger, taken by surprise in his nest of straw. He can't be comfortable there.

The Chatenays Talk About Him

I'm unable to fall asleep because the light is on. Henriette needs it to read by after her prayers. I can hear snippets of conversation float up

to me. My imagination takes off. I decide to go to the toilet to eavesdrop. Robert is talking. "He may only be sixteen, but he's big! A decent fellow who only asks to work!" The door slams and I hurry to bed.

The next morning, I can't resist the temptation to take a little trip to the barn. It's on my way to school. I'll keep my ears open for the bell that rings before the half-hour. Darn! The young man is gone.

I'm leaving the barn when Antoinette comes and blocks my path. "How many times do I have to tell you not to nose about without permission?" she asks, exasperated. I'm surprised because I thought she'd finished her work in the barn. "Don't you hear me when I speak to you?" she adds sternly. I shrug my shoulders. How would I know how many times I don't hear? But I don't answer.

"If you don't go to school right now, I'll find some work for you to do. Have you lost your tongue?"

"Uhhh, no, but I'm too early for school."

She runs out of patience. "Keep it up and you'll be late!"

"Fine, I don't care. If I'd known...."

"And on top of that, she talks back! You're not so free with your tongue when I ask you for information. Then you act like a baby. What are you waiting for? Go to school!" I start to cry in consternation. "This is no time to be blubbering. Get moving before I take my hand to you!"

Morning bells are ringing. I can hear the school bell. The door will be closed and I'll be punished, I'm sure. I have the impression that my schoolbag is heavier than usual. I'm going to get it.

Knock Hard

I walk slowly to school, praying to Our Lady. I stop in front of the sign that says "Knock Hard" and take a deep breath. They'll see that I've been crying and they'll laugh at me. I must be red as a beet. They'll make me stand in the corner and give me a bad mark. I'm trembling. I'll just have to run away across the orchards. I'll eat fruit that has fall-

en on the ground. I know how to milk a cow, I'll be able to drink milk. I won't die of hunger. I've decided – I'm leaving. I'll look for my parents and I'll find them. I want to go home!

I've failed. Antoinette the wicked stepmother stands in front of me, pointing at the school door like a weather vane. I'm trapped. We stare angrily at each other. My teeth are clenched. Oh, Mama, Mama! I try to be good, but I don't know how to anymore. Why should I be punished like this? How can I knock on the door? My tears are preventing me from seeing. I'm just a silly goose that nobody wants to help.

"What are you waiting for? For me to come after you?" yells my guardian. I really have no choice. I knock as hard as I can. Once. Twice. Three times. God, have pity on me.

His Name Is Bernard Hanau

He lives in the attic above the shed. His bed is against the wall of our toilet. He can hear us too because when I'm in there, I sometimes hear the tinny sound of his radio with its whistling, scratchy noises blurring the words. "My French compatriots! France in exile is speaking to the French!" One day when he was with Monsieur Chatenay, they were shouting for joy, "Hurrah! Hurrah!" I would have liked to be with them. Every evening, he comes back from work all dirty and has a glass of wine and leafs through the newspaper. He gives me a silent wink. I respond with a smile, which must please him because he cheers up. I think he senses that I'm waiting for him.

Bernard Hanau, a few years later, in an army photograph.

It's the Lord's Day

The sun is glorious! When it's time, I'm the first one ready. I'm very proud. There's nothing like it to put me in a good mood. I slip outside without saying anything to the family, who are all busy dolling themselves up to go to mass. Since Henriette has been singing in the church choir, she's been practising her music constantly. Every day, she does her voice exercises over and over.

Surprisingly dressed up in his Sunday best, Bernard Hanau, the farmhand, is standing with his legs apart and his hands in his pockets, staring into the clouds, and he doesn't see me. He seems lost in thought beyond the mountaintops of the Isère region. Walking very softly, I stand below his line of vision. This has become a habit. But this time, I cross my arms behind my back and take a little jump forward. And a miracle occurs – he smiles kindly at me.

"You can come closer, you know, I don't bite. Really!" That wasn't what I thought. Then he bends his long neck down until his face is level with mine.

"Would you like to fly through the air?" he asks me in a low voice, making a flying motion.

"Do you mean playing airplane?" I ask.

And without a word, he grabs my ankle in his right hand and my

wrist in his left one, and there we go for a flight through the clouds. "Bon voyage, little one!" He spins quickly, very quickly, very, very quickly and I fly up, down, up, down in a dizzying whirlwind of pleasure and illusion. The wind caresses my face and ruffles my hair. I feel light, as light as a feather. I could fly all the way to the stars.

"More?" asks a voice, bringing me back to earth.

"Yes! Faster than the merry-go-round!"

What was I thinking? All I can see is a soft mist and then, wham! a forced landing. I find myself sprawled on the floor of the cow barn. Things always have to go wrong. I cling to Bernard because it's not over, everything is still spinning – the house, the scenery, everything is upside-down.

"Are you hurt?" he asks nervously.

"I don't think so. But it smells awful."

"No wonder. You landed in a cow pie!" he says, opening his mouth wide in a big laugh.

"My sandals are disgusting, my bum is wet and my dress is dirty. How can I go to church now?"

"You just need to clean yourself up. It's not that bad. Don't worry about it." He starts laughing again. I mutter between my teeth, "I'm going to get a beating!" Bernard looks sad. "Do you want me to tell them it was my fault?"

"No!"

I stand up in one bound. I will surprise them, which I like to do anyway. I don't want to get him in trouble, it's not worth it.

"Did you know it brings good luck?" he says to cheer me up. "And we had a good laugh. I'll explain that it was an accident – in fact, that's the truth. Well, I have to go. Goodbye."

It's our secret, just the two of us. I haven't had that much fun in a long time. I run to the house and walk in, out of breath. The Chatenays look at me, stunned.

"Where have you been? What happened to you? Look at your dress!"

"It was slippery and I fell."

My sister is angry at me because she has to clean me up. She acts disgusted and dunks me in the cold water of the outdoor washbasin. I can't say anything, so I just have to put up with it. How could I have known I was going to fall? She does her martyr act and I wish she were in my place. She really

With Black, Vatilieu, 1943.

gives it to me, scrubbing and scrubbing me with the brush. I'm very uncomfortable but it's better if I don't say anything. "I have to clean your shit! You'll pay for this, young lady!" She acts like she's so grown up, making faces to show how much I'm putting her out.

The Chatenays now have a good reason for keeping me in the house, but I'm not sorry. Bernard is my friend and mine alone. I tell this to the dog, who knows how to keep his mouth shut. Black has replaced Choukette. I love them both.

A Surprise?

We go to church without Robert or Granny. They're both busy. After mass, Madame Chatenay decides to take a walk across the fields. It's poppy season, but I only gather daisies; the other flowers die too quickly. As I walk, I listen distractedly to my big sister talking. She's playing the intelligent young lady. I just let her go on. When we get to the farm, we find Monsieur Chatenay on the doorstep with blood on his shirt. He says there's a surprise waiting for us. "A surprise?" I  shout in astonishment. My sister gives me her accusing look. What did she want me to say? The words just came out.

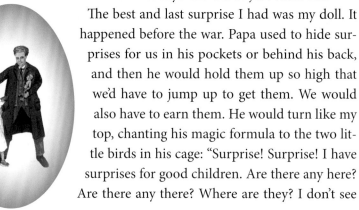 The best and last surprise I had was my doll. It happened before the war. Papa used to hide surprises for us in his pockets or behind his back, and then he would hold them up so high that we'd have to jump up to get them. We would also have to earn them. He would turn like my top, chanting his magic formula to the two little birds in his cage: "Surprise! Surprise! I have surprises for good children. Are there any here? Are there any there? Where are they? I don't see

them!" We'd get excited and search everywhere, turning every pocket inside out, exploring every fold of his coat. He would ask questions and we would answer with a yes or a no. He would want me to guess, and he'd help me more than Henriette.

And what if the surprise is... good God!... what if it's Papa? Papa, here waiting for us? Oh, my God! I have tears in my eyes. What a surprise that would be!

I follow the family blindly, clutching my bouquet so tightly that I crush the stems in my sweating hand. The procession stops at the stable. I beg you, Lord! Let it be him.

"Look! Come see the little calf! Isn't it adorable? Isn't it cute? Look at his mother, he looks just like her!" the Chatenays chorus. Then Robert says cheerfully, "Don't scare them, now. She's just given birth, our good girl, and she needs calm."

This is not at all what I was expecting. They go off to drink to the blessed event, with my sister following. I'd rather stay here with the ache in my heart. Upset and disappointed, I stretch my hand out to the innocent little calf, who isn't to blame for anything. I stroke it the way the hair grows, as Mama used to tell us to do with our dog. She would say, "Always stroke the way the fur grows, never against." I'm angry with her, but from time to time  when I'm asleep, I hear her whisper these words that haunt me: "Mar-gue-ri-ta-leh, mayneh beybeleh." And you, on your shaky legs, you let me run my fingers along your back. It reminds me of a song Papa sang about scratching a flea on your back. He always used to tickle me when he sang it.

Confession

When Henriette goes to confession, she makes up stories for the priest and then she's washed clean of her sins. This time, I hide in the corner  by the confessional before they go in and listen to her. She really lays it on. I admit that we're always fighting, but she says she's bitten me and beaten me up so many times. She's really exaggerating. She doesn't beat me up that much because I don't let her anymore. But that's not how she tells it to the priest. The liar will have to repent for what she's confessed. Unfortunately, I burst out laughing instead of running away. The two of them come out of the confessional. I shrink back as far as I can, but they see me.

"What are you doing there, you wretched girl?" the priest asks me. I look at them, filled with shame. Will I have to confess now?

"Me? Nothing. I was waiting for her."

"For how long?"

"The whole time."

"Well, good for you. Now it's your turn."

He takes me firmly by the arm and flings me down on the prie-dieu. That will teach me to listen at doors. I can't see his face when he asks, "What do you have to be sorry for, my child?"

"Maybe that I love to eat?"

"Don't you know, Marguerite, that listening at the door is a sin?" he says sternly.

I hesitate and then say pathetically, "My sister is a liar, I swear. Since I've started defending myself, she doesn't beat me up as much as before."

"So! You're not only a snoop, you're a tattletale too!" he says in an angry voice.

"I'm telling the truth," I insist rashly.

"And is that the only thing she does that's wrong?" he asks sarcastically.

I take advantage of the opportunity to add, in all seriousness, "No. She takes a diaper pin and sticks it in my doll's legs. And when I yell at her, she does it again. But she didn't tell you that."

"Good Lord, what a child! She doesn't see the error of her ways. Have pity on her soul. In the name of the Father, the Son and the Holy Ghost. Amen." He straightens up and looks me in the eye. "Our Father who art in heaven, hallowed be thy name..." I recite it along with him, making the sign of the cross as you're supposed to.

I'm ready to leave. But he stops me and makes me kneel on the ground like Jesus Christ in his suffering. "To punish you for your insolence, you'll have to go around the church on your knees." Oh, if only I could say I'm Jewish! I keep this thought in my head to console myself. I go forward slowly on the cold, hard floor. Before I've gone half way around, my knees are hurting. I'll never get to the end. There's nobody around. I look out the door, pluck up my courage and run all the way home.

Jacqueline Is Always Thirsty

In the last few days, the new girl in the village has started saying hello to us. She's our age and seems very nice. We've smiled timidly at each other. I showed her my doll and she showed me hers.

I'd really like to talk to her and get to know her. She's in my sister's class at school. She lives in the little house across the street with her mama. I wonder why they've come here. They don't have a lot of things, but they're not poor. Jacqueline has a nice pillbox, wears a lovely chain that shines in the sun and also a bracelet. The Chatenays told us they've taken refuge here, but they haven't said anything else. She and her mother don't talk much. When we meet every once in a while, I'm careful not to talk about religion, although I'd like to. When the neighbours go to church, they follow at a distance.

Sometimes the daughter comes to our place to do her homework with my sister. I sit at the end of the table because it's nice to work together. She's not allowed to run, it could kill her. Her mother gives her injections and controls her food. No candy. No cake. She only drinks water because of her diabetes. She drinks all the time. She never complains, but she's not very cheerful. When we skip, she always turns the rope. We play cards and dominoes when it isn't nice out, or else we play house. In our games, the father is always away at war and, of course, I'm always the baby.

What if We Called Them Papa and Mama?

Henriette has spoken to me seriously about the Chatenays. It's been over a year that we've been living with them. She proposed that we call them Papa and Mama for good and asked what I thought about that.

How can she burden me with this? What about our real Papa and our real Mama? I don't understand her. I agree that we should do it in front of people – but not for good. All my hopes are dashed. I don't feel like answering her.

"Yes or no?" she insists. I don't like her tone of voice or the way she orders me around just because she's the older one. If I say no, she'll get mad and if I say yes, I'll feel like a traitor. What will my parents think when they come back? She looks me in the eye and I'm thinking of them. She says, "Imagine, Marguerite! They'd be so happy. Why are you being such an idiot? You know they want to adopt us. We'll be baptised. And one day, you'll have your first communion in a long white dress like all the other girls. So, is it yes? Can we start tomorrow?" I don't answer, but she repeats, "Is it yes?" She shakes me so hard that I say, "Okay, do what you want, it doesn't matter to me."

"We'll both do it, when I give the signal."

At breakfast, torn between my shame and her pride, we lie, saying, "Thank you, Mama."

The next day, I go picking apples with Robert. I gather poppies and avoid addressing him. I listen to the sound of our steps and the creaking of the wheelbarrow. I think of my sister's words and of my love for Papa. I walk softly along the grass-lined path, wondering whether I have to give up the true to gain the false. I see myself far away from here, on our street in Paris before the war, in our shop near Monsieur Bieder's tailor shop, and I compare it with what I have now. I wish I could be elsewhere, at the age I was when my father would hold me and read me lovely stories in a low voice while turning the pages. I'd nestle my head in the hollow of his shoulder, and everything would be all right.

"Are you coming, child?" asks Papa Robert.

"My name is Marguerite!" I cry, upset.

Roussette Bolts

Time passes slowly while I wait for school to start again. Robert asks
me to watch the cows to keep me from quarrelling with my sister.
She's practising her scales for the church choir. She'd bathe in holy water if she could. The fields are green and welcoming. In the beautiful
sunshine, I walk among the cows – Fauvette and Noiraude, Émeraude
and Coquette – and we communicate with our eyes. They look at me
tenderly and comfort me. My "father" pats Roussette and I imitate
him.

The big animal is in calf and she's lying on her fleshy belly. When
my "father" goes away, I climb onto her. "You're my favourite!" I tell
her. I pat her gently, but she doesn't like it. I stretch out along her back

and put my cheek against the warmth of her neck, close my eyes and let my mind drift. I bask in the warmth of her body. Then I pretend I'm playing blind man's buff.

But Roussette gets angry and stands up and charges forward. In a flash, we pass "Papa," who looks stunned. "Don't be afraid, little one!" he cries. But before the words are out of his mouth, I'm already slipping, about to fall off the cow's back. I try to grab the end of her tail. But I lose my grip and fall onto the ground, to the amusement of the other cows who stand grazing, staring at me. I've learned my lesson: when cows are resting, leave them alone. You disturb them at your own risk.

The Part in the Middle

Lucky me, I will be given some yarn. Madame Chatenay is unravelling the sweater Robert tore. She starts with the body and goes up to the

sleeves, without losing any yarn. I stand patiently while she winds the yarn around my outstretched arms to form skeins. After a while, it's my turn to roll the yarn into balls. She busies herself in her grocery store while I'm doing it. The temptation is irresistible and I start juggling with the balls of

yarn. I go faster and faster.

"You'll get them dirty," scolds Granny, distracting me for a moment, and the balls of yarn fall to the ground. She gathers them and puts them in the basket. Now I'll have to pay for my mistake. To keep me from talking back, Granny shows me how to knit with the stiff yarn. One plain, one purl... I'm making the ribbing for a pullover.

I'm mad at Antoinette. I don't feel like calling her Mama when she bothers me. She's the one who decided that a part in the middle would suit me better. Instead of one ribbon, I have two. I didn't ask for that! I hardly recognize myself. I look strange and I don't like

it. This ridiculous hairdo makes my face look misshapen. At bedtime, without my even combing it, my hair goes to the right side. It's true what Mama said: you should never stroke an animal's coat the wrong way.

The Search

Near the end of the school day, we're disturbed by strange sounds that

upset me – sounds of tires on gravel, doors slamming, unnerving cries. I turn discreetly and look out the window. They're in front of our house! Maybe it's for us. I could try to hide under the teacher's desk, but I don't dare. Sweat runs down my forehead, yet I'm shivering and there's a drum beating in my chest. Some men in navy-blue uniforms turn the corner at the school. We're surrounded! I won't be able to escape. In my familiar distress, I run and hide behind the teacher so that they won't find me. It's my only hope.

There are a lot of black cars, one of them right in front of our house, and a truck. It's a trap. They're going to trap me like a rabbit

and put me in their prisoners' van. They take me out first, with one of them on either side of me. Mama is crying and Papa says, "When they question you, child, tell them the truth, tell them everything!" Once again, my parents abandon me.

A person leads me to the kitchen. What truth am I supposed to tell them? Are they soldiers? Are they policemen? They search everywhere, opening drawers, emptying shelves and cupboards, turning everything upside down. What are they looking for? Why is this one coming over to me? What does he want me to tell him? I'm paralyzed with fear.

"What's your name? Where do you come from? Where were you born? What did your parents do? Have you been here long? Are you Jewish?" I feel my cheeks getting warm. Who are they really, this band of brutes? Are they expecting me to tell them everything and turn myself in? To confess my hatred and terror? You won't get an answer from me, I'm not saying a word.

Antoinette is watching me. "Tell them, Marguerite! Tell them who you are! Tell them why you're with us! Do it for you and for us! If not, they'll take my Robert away and you'll be without a father for the second time. Tell them, I beg you!" She doesn't know what she's saying. I pity her, but still, I mustn't say anything.

There are more than twenty of them. They're jostling me on all sides. The soldier coming down the stairs looks nicer than the others. He takes me kindly by the hand and leads me outside, just the two of us. He looks at me and says, "I know your name is Marguerite, isn't it? It's a pretty name." I keep my teeth clenched. "You come from Paris and your parents were furriers there. Your sister told me. Don't be afraid, I'm from the Maquis, the Résistance. You must tell me everything." I don't say anything, I just nod my head each time. He couldn't have guessed it; Henriette must have turned us in.

Here she is, with reddened eyes, shouting, "Now nobody will believe us! They know who we are. What will become of us?"

Seeing Robert in front of the car, I point to him and manage to say, "You're not going to take him away?"

"We certainly are, but don't worry, we'll bring him back."

I've heard those words before.

The grandmother comes to get us to pray at Antoinette's brother's house across the road. They're all sitting there with their rosaries and we take our place at the end of the table amid subdued murmurs. I count the beads. The men from the *Maquis* speed away in their front-wheel-drive cars, taking this father away and leaving me in a fog of misery. The heartbreaking goodbyes of his wife remind me of a similar scene a long time ago, but I don't cry as much this time.

A few days later, they give Robert back to us.

Two Mamas

Coming into the house after school, I smell the aroma of cake. But I immediately sense that something is wrong. Granny is knitting her socks and doesn't say hello to us. "Mama's" red eyes and gloomy expression worry me.

In a caustic tone of voice, Antoinette declares, "Listen to me, girls. Your mother – yes, Madame Élias, in person – called me on the

phone. After nearly two years' total absence, after never answering my letters, back she comes, just when I was thinking of adopting you. And not only that, I discover that she's not crazy, contrary to what they had told me." She looks at the two of us with an expression that's both scornful and sad. Henriette has her head down. I'm upset by all this and I need to move around. Madame Chatenay looks at the clock. "Hurry, girls, in an hour, you have an appointment to meet her at Notre-Dame-de-l'Osier, across from my sister's house. My niece, Cécile, will go with you, I don't have the desire or the courage to go myself. To think that I kept you and took care of you as if you were my own daughters. In spite of the risks. And this is my thanks!"

I squirm with shame. "I hope they're not going to put us back in the convent," I plead in a low voice.

"That's not for me to decide anymore, my poor children. Your mother is not sick. And you won't have your communion," she adds to my sister. The hypocrite doesn't say a word. "Mama" finally motions to the pastry I've been coveting. "That's enough talk for now. Come taste my raspberry pie." It's so irresistible that I gobble up half a piece in one mouthful, but Antoinette jumps on me. "One minute, my girl! Where are your manners? Do you want your mother to say I haven't brought you up well?" I don't dare say anything. Soon, maybe it will be the other one who will be getting angry.

It's been so long since I've seen her, I'm afraid we won't recognize each other. It will be like blind man's buff, where you have to guess. That makes me feel terrible. I remember her black hair that she'd brush every morning before putting on her perfume and every night after undressing. We would smell her perfume from the stairs. She was so stylish, she wore such nice clothes. Antoinette gives us a second piece of pie, then wipes my mouth and takes me on her lap. Tears are running down her cheeks. I feel sad for her. Now I really can't call her "Mama." How could I? What would the other one say?

She does our hair and puts ribbons in it. "Do we have to take all our things?" asks my sister, the good student, already packing her schoolbag. Antoinette begins to sob. "I certainly hope not. That would be the last straw!" she answers, standing up. I had no mother and now I have two. It's very unpleasant.

Cécile, her niece, comes to get us. I'm shaking all over. They put us in the cart, but then Antoinette asks, "Haven't you forgotten something?" Yes. We haven't given her a kiss. Our unhappy "mother" picks me up and hugs me so hard that I ache all over.

The road is bumpy and our trip uncomfortable, especially because it's the cows that are pulling the cart. Soon we'll meet Mama. I'm eager to see her, but I'm also apprehensive. I look awful with my hair parted in the middle. The part on the right side suited me better. Here we are in front of Marie's house, Antoinette's sister. We have to remain here. Cécile will come and get us. She takes off the harness to let the cows

graze. I lean against the side of the cart watching my sister pace up and down. We don't say anything to each other.

"Look, here she comes! She's coming out. I see her! Mama! Mama!" she shouts, loud enough to wake the dead. She can't stand still, she's jumping up and down. I don't move. Mama didn't have a hairdo like that. She really does look crazy. Who is this person?

She throws off her cape, spreading her arms like Jesus

Christ on the cross, and says with her accent, "My little girls! My dear little girls!" Her model daughter rushes to her and throws her arms around her neck, talking non-stop and kissing her again and again. They don't need me and I don't care. They collapse onto the grass.

Finally, she calls me, "Margueritaleh! Margueritaleh!" I'm irritated and hesitate, then I run to her. She takes me onto her lap, moving the big one aside. "Come, mayneh beybeleh, you too, come and kiss dayneh mamaleh. You've grown! Don't you recognize me?" It's when she hugs me that I feel it's my mother. She has the same accent as Auntie. They can't speak French properly. But the more I hear her, the less it bothers me.

She takes some chocolate-covered shortbread cookies out of her shoulder bag and offers them to us, as many as we want. We laugh until we cry and we cry for joy. She gives her favourite a beautiful watch. Doesn't she realize I also know how to tell time? I weep with jealousy. She slips a package into my pocket: it's a tiny baby-doll wrapped in fabric. I don't want it but I thank her grudgingly. She explains that she had bought us beautiful chain bracelets engraved with our names. She wrapped them up in a handkerchief with her big gold spoon, her papers and her jewellery, but there was a *rafle* in Lyon when she was at the grocery store and she had to run, leaving her bag of food on the counter. When she went back ten minutes later, it was gone. "Thieves! Bandits!" she says angrily. But it was a close call. She could have been picked up and sent to the camps with all the other Jews. She cries into her handkerchief and I'm upset. Henriette is talking so much I can't get a word in, but everything she's saying is false. She talks about her life with the Chatenays and she makes it sound like she's Cinderella. As usual, she's exaggerating.

From the door of the convent, a sister calls, "Think of the children, I beg of you! It's seven o'clock." Already? I'm surprised. Mama starts to cry, with her frog eyes. "Goodbye, Henriettaleh! Goodbye, Margueritaleh! I'll see you very soon, my little girls." She kisses us quickly and she's gone, without saying when she'll come back. "Mama! Mama!" the two of us murmur at the same time. We go back to the Chatenays' on the bumpy road. We're sitting side by side. I'd rather keep quiet than talk to that liar.

Spring 1945, meeting at Notre-Dame-de-l'Osier (Isère).

Everyone Annoys Me

Antoinette has redone my hair with the part on the side. Since we saw Mama, Henriette constantly bosses me around. She doesn't know what she's saying anymore. She said too much against the Chatenays and I can't look them in the face anymore. She blames me for everything. I feel ill-at-ease and I'm completely confused. What will she tell the priest about her communion? How long will this reunion with our mother last?

Antoinette watches us and I'm so annoyed with Henriette the turn-coat. Oh, Mama, Mama! If you don't come back tomorrow, I don't know what I'll do.

My Linden Tree

From my bed, I see it swaying in the wind. Sometimes I hear birds in its branches. When the weather is good and I'm bored, I go and sit at the foot of my tree between the roots with my back against the trunk. It smells so good that I forget the torments I've suffered.

But, beautiful tree, this is my last time in your familiar shadow because I'm going away to Lyon. I'll no longer gather your flowers to make calming herbal tea. I've come to say goodbye to you. We're leav-

ing Vatilieu and I'm changing religions. I'll take a few leaves with me to remember the best linden tree ever! And I'm touching the wood of your trunk for good luck.

Since Mama's surprise visit, the Chatenays have been angry all the time. They pray more than usual in church and they don't care if I'm lonely. Is it my fault if they thought they would keep us till the end of their days? I will leave a small part of myself here. Henriette will become Papa's violinist. I've so often dreamed of waking up in Paris between him and my mother, with his arms around me. Then why am I sad that the war is over? To remember you, I'll sing Schubert's "Linden Tree." I learned it at school, in a classroom right next door to you.

By the fountain, near the ramparts,
there stands a linden tree.
While I was sleeping in its shadow,
sweet dreams it sent to me…

Goodbye, Chatenays

At the Vinay train station, they kept gazing lovingly at us. "So much has happened in the two years we've taken care of you. We got to know each other. Do you understand, girls? You were family!" I felt so uncomfortable that when they kissed me, I couldn't even wipe their tears from my face. I wanted to scream with rage, but I cried. I was upset and sad, and I didn't know what to think.

With my nose against the window of our compartment, I watch them disappear. I don't say anything. We don't need them anymore. From this moment on, they're no longer our parents. We must forget Vatilieu. Seated comfortably in our corner of the train, we can see the train driver not far from

us. I'm facing my sister, who's looking out at the mountains.

Goodbye, Chatenays! We're never coming back.

Part Three:

THE LONG ROAD HOME

1

2

1   Harry Vidékis with us in Lyon.

2   In Lyon, early 1945.

On the Train

The sister keeps her eye on us. I don't need her, she's not the person I was expecting. Mama was not at Vinay. Another snag. She'll meet us in Lyon. I'm disappointed. We had to sleep at the Notre-Dame-de-l'Osier convent. I refused to undress. We leave again with Estelle Évrard, who watches me constantly and talks about this and that, but only to Henriette. I'm longing for my parents.

The train is full of soldiers. I wish my father were among them. Almost everyone is asleep. I feel so alone. Facing us are a pair of soldiers wearing caps like Papa's, laughing like crazy. The first one grabs my doll, holds it between his knees and takes a cent from his pocket. Then he puts the coin against my baby's face and pushes

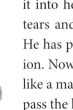

it into her eye! I turn away, my eyes filled with tears and I force myself not to cry out in rage. He has punctured the sweet face of my companion. Now, I can hear the little eye rattling around like a marble within its hollow body. The soldiers pass the half-blind creature from one to the next.

My tears are in vain because the barbarian takes a pen and draws black eyebrows and a moustache on its wounded face, saying, "Heil Hitler! It's a casualty of war!" He finally returns it to me after giving it a mocking salute. They all leave, laughing and shoving one another. I hug my poor mutilated doll with all the strength of my feelings and surround it with the warmth of my love, curling up on the seat with my hand under my head.

The Reunion

We say goodbye to the *micheline*, the little train between Vinay, the station in Vatilieu and Grenoble. We have to take another train with Mama and Simca, a short, mischievous-looking little man I don't

know. The train we need to get to is quite far away from the platform we are on. We're warned that we can't miss it so the four of us run. "Come on, hurry up!" they keep repeating.

We're finally in the train and I'm completely out of breath. People are pushing and shoving. We weave our way from car to car, looking for seats and a place for our baggage. But we have to stand. Luckily, it won't be for long.

We change to a tram for the first and last time. It's half-empty and much slower. Nobody bothers me, so I take a short nap. Suddenly a voice shouts from a loudspeaker, "Everyone must get off!" I awake with a start and stand up, fearful and ready to flee. But I stop in my tracks – at the end of the electric cables of the tramway, I see sparks shining in the sky! A man's voice asks, "What are you waiting for, little girl?" There's traffic coming from both directions and I'm afraid it will hit me. Simca takes my arm and drags me behind him to make me go faster.

All the hotels are full and we're laden down like mules and completely discouraged. Finally, there's one with a room. "Follow me, ladies and gentlemen!" bellows the fat innkeeper, her cheeks as red as tomatoes. We climb the stairs in single file, without stopping. I'm panting a little. "There are two more floors," the innkeeper announces, not thinking of our baggage. I can't go on, but I do anyway. Finally, we reach our room. I collapse onto the first bed and fall asleep with exhaustion.

Who turned on the light? There's someone snoring behind me. I sit up and discover that I'm sharing my bed with a naked animal. It's Simca and he's very hairy! But the worst thing is seeing my Mama in the other bed holding her favourite daughter tenderly in her arms. Henriette's eyes are wide open. "I asked first!" she says nastily. I'm so angry that I leave the room and go walking in the hallway.

It's Not Fun in Lyon

We're living upstairs at Madame Pfeiffer's. There isn't much to do and her son scolds me every day. I liked it better at the Chatenays'. Mama is working for a furrier. During the hours of waiting, I pass the time by taking apart, cleaning and reassembling the old alarm clock she's given me to repair. Now it works perfectly, for which I have received compliments. Henriette reads all day, ly-

ing on our bed. She doesn't play with me anymore and I think I know why. Our young sitter only leaves his office to eat and sleep, without a friendly smile or a word to us. We mustn't both-er him, his father was massacred. He was in the *Résistance*, like both our mothers. In his presence, I feel his sadness.

The women are in mourning and they often weep. When Mama speaks of going out, I try to make her stay. When she stays in, all she does is cry. In the evening, they go to meetings. I don't want to stay in Lyon because I can't go out by myself. It seems that lost children are stolen in the streets and later found murdered or poisoned with candies.

I wander around the apartment. I could breathe freely in Vatilieu, where I had plenty of space, al-though I missed my parents. I could gather the beautiful fruit in the orchards in my lovely wil-low basket without having to be afraid of men.

It doesn't seem like the war is over. Mama comes home after midnight, too tired to talk. There's no shower here, not even a tub. Mama scrubs, rinses and dries us stand-ing on a towel beside the kitchen sink. I miss the shower in the Chatenays' house. I wish we could leave here.

My mother goes out every morning. Luckily, there's the cat for me to cuddle with. I fill his bowl with milk and I clown around – he seems to enjoy it. When I sit down to read or draw, or when I'm completely discouraged, he climbs up on the table, puts his face against my forehead and purrs to me.

On My Knees

Maybe Monsieur Pfeiffer wouldn't have died if his family still prayed. A sister in the convent taught me that if I begged the Lord regularly, Papa would come back. So I'm practising in secret. Every morning while eating my breakfast, I pray in silence. Every night, when no one can see me, I pray again. Without a sound, I recite the whole "Hail Mary" because God takes pity on those who deserve it.

Little Red Riding Hood

I know the story by heart. I've told it to my doll while thinking of Papa, who read it to me several times so that I would understand it.

He'll be glad to hear me read it so well. Sitting in his lap, I was less afraid of the wolf. We were in the corner of the living room on the fur-covered hassock.

When I'm reading and bare my teeth and shout, "The better to eat you with, my child!" guess whose voice I hear? My father's.

Cats!

Mama is out again and I'm awakened by piercing cries. There are children crying in the street and I'm afraid. "Henriette! Do you hear them?"

"Stop bothering me! Let me finish my book, I only have a chapter left," my sister answers, irritated. As for the Pfeiffer boy, he's half-asleep and doesn't hear me. I climb up onto the toilet seat and look out the window. Right in front of me are a lot of tiny lights pointing at me, like an army ready to attack! I've never seen so many cats on the edge of a roof. With their tails in the air and their claws extended, they could jump on me! I get down very quickly. The cries begin again. So it was them howling, fighting over a bowl of milk. I escape to the kitchen to listen to the radio. A key turns in the door and I recognize the voices of my mother and Madame Pfeiffer talking softly. I go and lie down in the darkness, reassured to know that Mama is home.

We're Going Back to Paris!

Tomorrow, the three of us will finally be in Paris to greet Papa. Mama has gone out with Madame Pfeiffer. It's her last meeting with her friends from the *Résistance*. I'm dying to see him, but this is no time to act up. Henriette has started talking to me again. We talk quietly together the way we used to. We mustn't wake people up. I imagine us in our court-

yard, at home for good. We'll get Choukette back and every Sunday afternoon we'll play our favourite games. Dear God, I promise, if you grant my wish, I'll never fight with my sister again. There are still eight hours to go before we leave.

The Seals

We are finally going to rue de Charonne, to our store. I want to see the neighbours again, and Georgette – but not the concierge or Monsieur Gellé. I want to forget *them*. Uncle Wolf is driving us there in his beautiful car. My heart is filled with hope. An officer from the *Résistance* is coming with us, to defend us if necessary. Mama takes me onto her lap, although I would rather sit on the seat, and she's holding me tight enough to smother me. From the car, I see merry-go-rounds and dream of being on them.

I recognize the area. Place de la République, with the statue of Marianne, and the park, and then boulevard Voltaire, where we used to walk before the war. We pass the Oberkampf métro station, the Bataclan theatre and then Saint-Ambroise Church. "The beautiful  church!" I say, without thinking. "Don't say that!" answers my mother harshly. It's the same thing with the catechism – we're not allowed to mention it anymore. Place Voltaire, the Mairie of the 11th arrondissement, the policemen with their revolvers. And there's the public urinal. I remember its nauseating smell. I would pick Choukette up so that she wouldn't follow my father into it. And then we'd go along the sidewalk on a bicycle, with me clinging to Henriette, and Papa following us to the bank with the dog. It all comes back to me as if it were yesterday. So why does it make me so nervous? Charonne métro station! We turn right. Sitting in the car, I'm quivering with emotion – we're in front of our house!

Standing in front of the huge gate, I'm shaking all over. I let the others go ahead of me, like the good little girl I am. I count to three and dash into the courtyard. We're home!

There's an iron bar across the door to our apartment. The landlord

provides an explanation, but he's clearly astounded to see us again. Fidgeting on the paved stones, at the very spot where I used to have tea parties with Hélène, I raise my head. There are curtains in her windows. The only thing missing is the sound of her piano. If only she could be there. Mama plays with her keys during an animated conversation with Monsieur Gellé. I wait, impatient to go up to the apartment. I'm eager to be home and find my toys, my dolls, my store, our telephones – the pretend one and the real ones. I wish my father would call me for real from where he is – I want to hear his voice in my ear. I want my top. I want my pedal car. I'll be able to ride around as much as I like.

I hear steps on the main staircase. The concierge is coming down with a boy and a girl, staring at us in amazement. "They're back! They're back!" she shouts, as if she were calling for help. Mama turns around and says accusingly, "No thanks to you, you vicious gossip! You'd be better off not saying anything!" And she spits on the ground. Anxious, I tug on her arm. I also turn around.

"Hello!" "Hello!" "Hello!" "Hello!" Monsieur Gellé's office staff greet us through the windows. A young man comes out of the factory and heads for the café. As he passes me, he says a friendly "Hello, there!" the way he used to before. It's Marcel, the boss's son. He's also surprised to see us. Did he ever used to get scolded by his father!

"Come, children," says Mama, turning toward us. "There's no point trying to fight Monsieur Gellé's unwillingness," she observes bitterly. "We'll come back tomorrow. I'll have to start working again if he wants to get his rent money! Even by collaborating, he couldn't have gotten the equivalent of three years' rent!" Leaning on his cane, Monsieur Gellé smiles as he walks away. Mama pulls me toward the street. Oh, how heartbroken I am! We wait in the car while Uncle and the officer continue to talk with Monsieur Gellé. But he's got a thick head.

We drive slowly to Place Voltaire. On the left, I see the Gaumont theatre, where we used to go to the movies with Papa on Saturday night. And there's the little park in front of the Mairie, where we were forbidden to go. We continue on to Porte Saint-Martin, Strasbourg-Saint-Denis and then rue Notre-Dame-de-Nazareth, where we stop in front of number 67. It's about time. I'm starving! I feel as if I could eat a whole loaf of bread as I climb the stairs to the third floor and I can't wait for Auntie to open the door. Finally I see her lovely smile. The tempting smell of food further sharpens my appetite. They seat me between Monique and Riri. The old painting of the countryside is reflected in the mirror over the mantelpiece. The farm in it looks like the one in Vatilieu. Tomorrow we'll take the same route, retracing our steps back. This time, we'll stop at the park, like the other children. Every day, I think about my father coming back, but I wait and wait and wait.

At Auntie Sonia's

The telephone rings. Auntie answers. She speaks in a low voice, but all of a sudden, "Rachel! Rachel! It's for you. You can go home!" The day is starting off well. Mama prefers not to say anything to us. She gets up, avoiding touching us so that she won't wake us up. I'm pretending to be asleep. I've learned to pretend without it showing. Tomorrow I'll sleep at home, rue de Charonne. I'm filled with joy! We don't have enough room here, with the three of us in Riri's bed. He's in Monique's bed, which is even smaller. But for a four-year-old and a six-year-old, it's big enough. It's not very comfortable with Henriette and Mama, but we manage.

Every night, Uncle opens up the grandmother's folding cot and sets it up in the corner of the dining room. His mother is as old as the Chatenays'. She hardly speaks any French. She's been living with them since her husband was deported with his youngest sister, Yvette, the one who was so nice to me when she used to take care of us at family celebrations. She'd give us as much cake and candy as we wanted and I'd stuff myself. She'd let us play "Ring around the Rosie." Ginette, the eldest, escaped to Switzerland with her husband. How would we have managed if they had been here too?

Everyone is talking at the same time. And in the racket, I hear Mama cry, "The seal has been removed! I'm going to be able to work, to earn money! But first, I have to go back there and check and sign the papers." She hugs us. I can already hear Papa shouting from the doorway, "And what about me? Don't I count?" I feel like singing the song I've practised for him – "Little Papa, it's your birthday today.

Mama has told me you're away" – but the words in my head are different: "Mama said you'd be back to stay. I've waited for you night and day."

My aunt is busy with the housework and taking care of my cousins. They're not very well behaved, they're little devils. Last night, I had so much fun with Riri. We were having a pillow fight, but they made us stop. Unfortunately, Uncle had left with his car – we would have needed it again. He went

Winter 1944, Sonia, Riri and Monique.

to paint a client's apartment. I remember the wallpaper he put up in our bedroom, with roses all over it. I remember all the treasures kept in the cabinet with the big drawers: my toys, my clothes. I'm so happy I'll be sleeping at home tonight!

There Are No More Arrests

The Germans have gone, not a minute too soon. We can walk freely in the streets and take the métro with no risk of being arrested and

taken away, as people were in the August roundup, which we narrowly escaped by quickly crossing the street. I remember the soldier holding up a sign ordering people to stop.

To show that I can read, I call out the métro stations. It makes Mama smile. "Strasbourg-Saint-Denis." We get off to transfer to the line going to Montreuil. We're not the only ones waiting for it. We get on and quietly take our seats. "République." That's where the dentist wearing the star was, who hurt me so much when he pulled my tooth. "Oberkampf." It's already less crowded. "Saint-Ambroise." A man with a frosty gaze stares at me. He looks like someone from the *Milice*, the militia. I shrink against Mama, who tenderly protects me. I announce, "Voltaire." We'll be getting off at the next stop.

"Are you ever going to shut up?" asks Henriette ill-humouredly. "Don't you see you're getting on our nerves?" I push her away. She ought to mind her own business. She should be the one to shut up.

I continue, louder than ever, pronouncing each syllable distinctly: "Cha-ron-ne!" "Stubborn as a Breton," Georgette used to say. Henriette gives me a look, but I don't care. Suddenly I see myself before we left Paris, when my sister shoved me as we were getting off the métro and made me fall on the platform. I don't dare go out the door until Mama takes my hand. We follow the crowd. I shiver.

"Exit. It's this way," says my big sister. We climb the stairs and get to the top out of breath. We go outside. It's warmer now. We cross the street and our shop is a bit further to the right.

I'm so happy to be going back home. But we have to wait in the courtyard until Mama comes back with the landlord. He doesn't even say hello. He takes his time opening the door for us. Then he walks away, limping. "To hell with him!" says Mama, walking into the apartment. I follow her with my heart pounding.

There's Absolutely Nothing Left

Where is the carpet on the stairs with the metal rods on every step? Mama is lost in a litany of lamentations. I move away from a spider web I've walked into. The apartment is filled with the smell of mould emanating from the kitchen. "There's nothing here anymore, it's empty!" exclaims Mama, ashen. "There's nothing but stinking garbage! I can't believe it!" Mama moans and heads for my room. "Filth!" Just hearing her, I'm afraid to go in. What will I find there? It's a disaster, a real disaster. The room is unrecognizable. It's been ruined. My legs give way and I feel as if I'm going to faint. What will become of us? Whole sections of the wallpaper have been torn off. The floor is warped. The door of the cupboard where I used to keep my dolls is hanging crookedly, with not even the smallest doll inside. The lock has been torn off. There's no point looking any further, there's nothing left. It's a nightmare. I pinch myself to make sure I'm not dreaming. But no, the evidence is in front of my eyes. I weep in dismay. I catch my foot in a hole in the floor. There are holes everywhere. "You'd think they were searching for treasure," says Mama, shaking her head over our poor apartment.

We go to the other side of the landing, hoping that the living room has been spared. The key to the door is missing. That was the room I used to sleep in before Papa's arrest. My parents slept on a sofa-bed and we slept behind a curtain at the end of the room. It was so lovely. It was home. It was nice living there. What's going to happen now? Where's the furniture from our apartment? It's a forlorn place now. The walls of the main room are dirty. The floorboards creak beneath our feet. Mama bursts into sobs, saying, "The swine! It's unbelievable! The place is not fit to be lived in." I can't bear her crying and muttering, "Oy vey iz mir... Oy, oy, oy vey iz mir... Gott in himmel! Voss hostu undz gemakht?" (God in Heaven! What have you done to us?) She's hunched over, rocking back and forth, moaning. I don't want to hear her. I don't want to understand.

Mama and Henriette talk quietly to each other. And I suffer another blow – Henriette is sitting on Mama's lap and they're holding each other. I clench my fists. The window is slightly open and I go over to it. I look out through the closed shutters without speaking. The shoe-maker's shop is closed, and so is the tailor's, for the same reason as ours. People pass by as if nothing is out of the ordinary. Why should they care? It doesn't concern them, they're not the ones who've been robbed. They're all cheats and collaborators! They've stolen my mem-ories and they've taken away all my hope.

While they go through the workshop and the store, I go out into the courtyard to get some fresh air. I walk all around it. Mama gives the keys back to the concierge. That one really irritates me, with her prying questions. We used to say she was a busybody. I cannot forget that she did everything she could to get us deported. And she still wants to gossip? Mama gives her some instructions. I turn my back but the hypocrite calls out, "Hello, Marguerite!" I'd rather be rude than answer her.

We walk to the métro station. The florist's daughters see us from behind their window. They're surprised and they call their father, that collaborator! They were the ones who locked me in the toilet at school and who pushed me into the gutter. I still have a bad taste in my mouth from it. My mother gives them a terrible look and says, "You despicable traitors! You'll be dealt with!" I'm ashamed in front of the onlookers who have gathered. I think of the story of Monsieur Seguin's little goat who fought right to the end. How brave and coura-geous it was. Why am I so fearful? We take the métro back toward Pont de Sèvres. I can't wait for this day to be over.

At night, in spite of everything, I pray, "Make Papa come back!"

Another Convent?

When we get back, the women start talking among themselves. It's about us. The telephone keeps ringing, why don't they pick it up? Nobody is allowed to disturb them, not even to ask for something to eat. We have to watch Monique and Riri. Henriette pretends she's the mother and we have to obey everything she tells us. My thoughts are elsewhere, far from here, in a despair that's still vague. I take my doll and lie down on the bed. My mother joins us at around midnight. She's packed our suitcase and put it in the hall. She goes to sleep without saying goodnight.

I'm awakened by the ringing of the telephone and the commotion in the apartment. Who's calling us so early? Why? I'm afraid of what

my mother and Auntie have decided. They never ask our opinion. Auntie stuffs us with treats while avoiding our gaze. No matter what she says or does, it doesn't make me feel less depressed. I choose not to say anything. I sulk. I'd rather not hear what's being planned. I take refuge in the bedroom with my hands covering my ears. I'm already expecting bad news. It's always the same thing.

The three of us leave in the car with Uncle, like animals going to slaughter. We're going to a boarding school in Fontenay-aux-Roses, near Paris. I don't listen to the explanations Mama gives us. Her telling us why does not make me feel any better. She says she has no other option right now. That she'll come see us very often, almost every Sunday. And that we'll be back home for the holidays. I don't believe a word of it. She's smiling pathetically, which shows she's lying to us.

At the sight of the huge crucifix, I realize that this is, yet again, a convent. I start trembling

again. "Don't worry, Marguerite, the sisters know you're Jewish. And I promise I'll come to see you." She takes out her handkerchief. I look at her, distraught. It's the same thing all over again. What was the point of making us tear up the pages of the catechism if we were going to be sent back to Catholicism?

Mama and Uncle kiss us hastily because the mass is about to begin. They repeat, "We'll see you soon!" I can't control my sobbing, but to hurt them I recite the Lord's Prayer in front of the sister. Mama cries and Uncle wipes his eyes and the Mother Superior says, "Amen!" Then she leads us, like orphans, toward incense and discipline.

Whooping Cough

I'm not allowed to take my doll to bed with me because the other children might be jealous. I don't feel well, but nobody understands why. For several days, I stay in the infirmary with my sister, who is very ill. It turns out that we both have  whooping cough. I can't stop coughing and have a high fever. The disease is contagious, so I'm kept in isolation and watched day and

 night. Henriette is so sick that they've had to take her to the hospital. She was vomiting blood and her face was burning. If she knew how much I miss her, she might try to come back here. I would help her get better. But if she died, would they tell me? I feel terribly alone and miserable.

Mama didn't come last Sunday. She's already forgotten me. And what if Papa has come home to work without being disturbed? And what if he was having breakfast with Mama beside him,

sharing his coffee and croissants? On this sunny day, I feel completely abandoned. I listen to the silence of the emptiness and I feel nothing but absence.

I wish I could fly out the window and go back to the Chatenays. I'd be better off in Vatilieu than here.

Monsieur Élias Is in the Parlour

"There is a Monsieur Élias in the parlour," a voice calls from the loud-speaker in the corridor. "Marguerite Élias is asked to come to the par-lour. Marguerite Élias, please come to the parlour," the voice repeats and my heart begins to pound. The whole class is listening. The whole class knows it's about me. The whole class except me, sitting frozen in place.

"Isn't that your name?" asks the teacher. I've lost my place in my book, I'm drifting in a dream – could it be pos-sible? I've said so many prayers to see my Papa

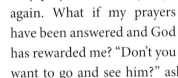

again. What if my prayers have been answered and God has rewarded me? "Don't you want to go and see him?" asks the sister in sur-prise. I remain seated with all eyes fixed on me, ill at ease, lost in emotion. What to say, what to do? "Marguerite Élias is wanted in the parlour." I can't believe it. The noise around me increases and someone takes off my smock. "Come back to earth!" cries the sister impatiently. She shakes me out of my stupor and pulls me by the hand.

I go forward fearfully. "Don't be afraid, child!"

My tears begin to flow when I reach the door to the office. I go in and stop cold. "No! No, it isn't Papa, it's Uncle! They lied to me!" I'm upset.

"Don't you recognize me?" pleads Uncle Léon, holding his arms out to me. "How you've grown!" He hugs me and kisses me tenderly on the cheeks. Then he takes me on his lap, saying, "Come here, I have something to tell you. I was a prisoner. I've just been released. I met your mother at the hospital, where I saw Henriette. Things are very bad. They're giving her blood transfusions and she sleeps in an oxygen tent. It hurts to see her. Your mother won't be coming today, but she'll probably be here next week. She gave me this parcel for you. Aunt Rose sent you this, look – a chocolate bar and shortbread cookies. Do you want one?"

"No, it's Papa I want. He didn't keep his promise. I don't want anyone but him. You're making me cry, can't you see? You don't understand! Nobody understands. I hate everyone!"

The Mother Superior suggests that he leave. He looks sad. I'm still in a state of shock. "Everyone tries to trick me! You're all liars. There isn't any God," I sob. "Have pity on her soul," says the sister, raising her eyes to heaven. She takes me with her and has me lie on my bed. Then she kneels and prays. She asks me, "What can I do to get a little smile from you?"

"Give me back my doll that they took away."

"All right. I'll bring it to you if you calm down."

She goes away and comes back a few minutes later with my doll. "You see? A nap will do you good." The bell rings, it's time to go to the dining room. Clutching my only link with my Papa to my breast, I drift off in spite of my distress. I was cruel to Uncle, I didn't even say thank you to him. I hear thunder receding in the distance, getting softer and softer. The hum of a sewing machine brings back the sound Mama's machine used to make.

My Last Prayer

Henriette is out of the hospital and I'm a lot better. Thank you, God – no more convents! Before school starts, we're going for a vacation in the country for a month. We have to gain weight. And after that, we'll go back to the house. As for prayers, "Forgive me, Father, but I mustn't say them anymore. The war is over and I'm Jewish, you understand? All that's missing now is Papa. So I'm begging you on my knees one last time to bring him back to me. You can do everything, so make him come home to us and never again be taken away from me. Goodbye, Our Father who art in heaven. I'm finally leaving this convent. You have almost given my mother back to me. Don't forget my Papa. This is my last prayer."

Another Hand-Me-Down Dress from My Big Sister

For the close to three years that we've been living apart from our mother, she hasn't been able to take care of our clothes and they're dirty and worn. I've complained, but nothing changes. When they're too small, I wear them anyway. I get hand-me-downs from Henriette, with holes and stains. There's no point discussing it. Henriette explains where the stains came from, but that doesn't make them go away. She gets new ones for holidays or the start of school, but I don't. And when we get used clothes, she

puts them on before I do and mocks me. I get the old ones. Luckily, my feet are bigger and more intelligent than hers, and won't go into her shoes – and my hands won't go into her gloves. When someone lends or gives me clothes, I'm careful to keep them in good condition. Unlike some people, I don't spoil my things. I take care of them.

In Quarré-Les-Tombes

The name alone sends chills down my back, but that's where we're going. What kind of people live in Quarré-les-Tombes? We'll know soon. The seats of the bus are filled with ashen-faced children between the ages of eight and fourteen. There are lots of boys. There's a lady with us, sitting near the driver. We cross the countryside amid

trees and flowers. Henriette is sleeping on our baggage. She didn't eat her breakfast – that won't do her health any good.

When we get to the village, there's a crowd of people waiting for us. I take a deep breath and get out, surrounded by kids. They've all been well-behaved.

People look at us tenderly while we line up in order of height. I stay as close as possible to my sister so that we can be together. Three times I refuse to go to a family that wants to separate me from her. The line quickly gets shorter and nobody wants to take the two of us together. The lucky ones who have been chosen form groups and then scatter. They each have a family to stay with. The lady accompanying us gives me a reassuring wink because I have good reason to worry now that we're the last ones left. Are they going to send us back to where we came from?

The nice lady comes back and, without any explanation, leads us to a house. She knocks on the door very loudly. They take a long time to answer. Finally, we're greeted with a smile by a couple – but I can't believe how old they are! "They're the oldest people in the village. You'll have to be very obedient," the lady tells us.

The grandfather mumbles, "Because of my age, I had the honour and the pleasure of ringing the bells of our victory against the Boches at the Liberation." I breathe a sigh of relief – he hates the Germans.

His wife adds, "Things always work out in the end. You must never give in." Unfortunately, they are hard of hearing and we have to shout to make ourselves understood. They can't hear that Henriette is still coughing. But they seem so nice, so obliging, that we adopt them right away.

They have three rabbits in a hutch in the yard. There are chickens and baby chicks and a goose. I feed them, calling, "Here, chickie, chickie!" the way I used to at the Chatenays'.  The situation isn't that different here; we're with strangers again. For our next meal, we're going to have rabbit stew. But when it comes time to kill it, I no longer want to eat it. The big one wiggles its nose. The white one has fur like my coat. And the grey one is so little. "This one," decides grandfather. "It will be delicious with white wine," he says, grabbing it by the back of the neck. The poor thing wriggles as much as it can. I pet it the way the fur grows, as you're supposed to. I see the hammer in the old man's hand. He takes the rabbit and hits it. I run away, far away, before the cook finishes it off with her knife.

His Honour the Mayor himself received us and made it clear that we're not staying with just anybody. Not knowing what to answer, I just grimaced.

Henriette spends almost all her time reading, sometimes sitting up but often lying down. There aren't many distractions, but it's better than at the boarding school. When it rains, we play dominoes and when it's nice, we play leapfrog or jump rope. One thing is certain: we avoid fighting.

My sister sets the table and I clear it. She washes the dishes and I dry them carefully. At sundown, I start feeling sad, but breathing in the smell of the blanket makes my chest swell with

happiness. I've come to like the smell of the mothballs

that we used to use to protect our furs. At night, I dream that my parents are at home and are very poor, that they abandon us in the forest like Hansel and Gretel. I awake with a start and try to go back to sleep. With all the lies I've been told, I have a hard time falling asleep. Things are all mixed up in my head and strange visions haunt me – Mama bent over her machine in a cloud of smoke, Papa crying somewhere, I don't know where he is or how long he's been there. They're everywhere and nowhere and I desperately need to find them.

We Finally Go Back Home

I'm so happy! We're going home for good with my aunt in Uncle's car. Sonia explains to us why Mama isn't here. "The dead season is over and work has started up again. There will be money coming in again."

In the meantime, they've given us new pyjamas – both of us, for once! Mine are nicer because they're blue.

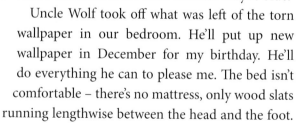

Uncle Wolf took off what was left of the torn wallpaper in our bedroom. He'll put up new wallpaper in December for my birthday. He'll do everything he can to please me. The bed isn't comfortable – there's no mattress, only wood slats running lengthwise between the head and the foot. We have no chairs or table. It's not fun eating standing up, but it's better than sitting on miserable boxes. There's no mirror to do my hair, so I have to look at myself in a pane of the window. There's not even a curtain to protect us from the prying eyes of the concierge. Mama has lost all hope. Dressed in black, as thin as a rake, she sleeps in an armchair someone has loaned her. But she isn't in mourning, is she?

Contrary to what had been planned, we won't be staying here after the summer. I'm more and more disappointed. Mama broke a glass every day and wished for my father's return, but he hasn't come back. It's very discouraging. My prayers didn't do any good either. She salvaged an old machine for sewing fur. She got back our silver-plated cutlery and the two picture frames stuffed with papers she had entrusted to Madame Graziani, which are hanging in the living room again. My sister doesn't play her violin anymore. Mama cries as she sews on the machine. I wonder what she's thinking about. She takes us to rue Vieille-du-Temple. There are mainly women and children there. One of them sets a good example by politely introducing himself. "My name is René Goldman. What's yours?" Without any parents, he seems more lost than we are. When he leaves, he calls, "See you at the next meeting!" I smile at him. Now we're signed up to go somewhere – I don't know where.

It's Not True

It's not true, my father has not been murdered in the Auschwitz concentration camp. He has disappeared and he'll come back soon. I watch for him, leaning out the window. The letter doesn't mean anything. It isn't real; it's as false as our baptismal certificates. He's surely a prisoner somewhere. It's all a lie.

Maybe he escaped to Lithuania, where he lived before coming to Paris, with our grandmothers, grandfathers, uncles and aunts, and all our cousins. We have lots of them. Mama has spoken of them so often. I remember the photographs Papa would spread out on his desk. His is looking at me now and I tell him I'm waiting for him. I'll always wait for him.

Henriette is sick because of it and has to stay in bed. I carry my pain back and forth in the empty apartment, clutching my doll that Papa gave me at the beginning of the war. My mother no longer believes in lucky charms. She sighs while she works and says over and over that there's no hope anymore. She's forgotten her promise and wants to get rid of us. Her smoke fills the room; she really smokes a lot. She says that while we wait for things to get better, she's going to send us to a place called Andrésy at the beginning of the school year. I'm afraid she may really be crazy because she stuffs us with candy. We're going to a house for children of people who've been deported to the camps – for orphans! My Mama doesn't understand anything. I'm not an orphan. I don't need fresh air, I need her, and I have to be here when Papa comes back.

I really resent it. We'll be leaving soon. It doesn't matter where we go if my parents aren't there. Nothing could be better than being at home. Why did she promise? My face is wet with tears. Uncle takes our suitcases and I leave, walking backwards to admire our old house.

I'll mourn until his return and mine.

I'm coming, Mama! I'm coming! I'm coming! I'M COMING!

Andrésy

In Andrésy, we live in the Manoir de Denouval, a beautiful mansion. It would be the perfect place if we needed to hide again. It's so complicated that it took me a while to be able to find my way around. Exploring it with our room-mates, we discovered a room full of toys. Luckily, we didn't get caught and we can keep a secret. To prevent them from hearing us, we smothered our laughter with our hands. Maybe we'll go back there later because we're dying to open up the packages. In the meantime, I have to keep the secret.

At the centre of the mansion is the huge room where we do our homework, eat our meals and listen to talks by the counsellors or guest speakers. On Saturday night, everyone gets dressed nicely. After supper, the older ones move the tables to the side and the benches to the front. We sit on the benches or the floor – we're not afraid of the cold, we keep warm by sitting close together. And we sing revolution-ary songs – "Let's not fear the weight of the stones, let's not fear the cold hard earth…" – and the "Partisan's Song" – "Through the valleys, over the mountains" – and the one I like better – "Comrade Lenin has died but his name lives on…" I also like "Brave soldier, back home from the war…," which reminds me of my father. I have a weakness for sad songs, and I know a lot of them. Before every meal, we sing, "Around a table with good friends, how nice to be together…," and at the end of the meal, "Thank you for your company, and for the food that we have eaten." It's more joyous than the prayers at the convent, and our voices ring out loudly.

On the Way to School

We have to get up early in the morning to go to school. We cross the garden in groups of three, all together. You can hear us shouting from miles away. "My girl, do you hear the sounds of the city?" We even shout in Yiddish, "Mir kumen on! Mir kumen on!" (We're coming! We're coming!) We follow the river, admiring the barges along the

way. Even when it's raining, we sing, "The sky is blue." And when we're tired, we sing, "On the mountains so high," which has a slower rhythm.

The bigger kids don't slow their pace for the smaller ones. I have to run to get there before the bell. I'm so exhausted that I'm half asleep during class and I don't know what's going on. When the teacher asks me questions, I never know the answers. I'm behind in my work. Henriette hardly ever comes to see me, let alone help me. I do my homework all alone. I'm always eager for the day to end, because I'm not a good student anymore.

I wish I could lie on my bed all day, but I know it's not allowed. On Thursday, I saw my sister with "Carrot-Top" – she was in his arms and they were looking into each other's eyes and kissing each other's cheeks. She spends her time with this boy instead of doing her work. I haven't seen Mama for a very long time and I'm starting to get worried again.

Mama Is Here!

It's Sunday. And it's sunny! We go for a picnic by the water with Mama. She's brought a camera. We sit on a blanket and nibble sweet treats.

When she talks to us about the nice gentleman who's been helping her in the workshop, a musician who was a prisoner of war, I can't stop myself from asking, "And what about Papa?" She answers that Papa is dead and I get angry. Next week she's going to introduce him to us. His name is Ary. She's told him that her daughters are nice and well-brought-up, and we're going to have to prove it.

When she leaves after showering us with wet kisses, I'm so sad that I fly into a rage. I hate her! I gobble up my half of the cheesecake she brought us, although it gives me indigestion. That will be her punishment. When I suffer, I get hungry. I throw up everything I've eaten. My stomach is sick. Mama has found someone to replace Papa. Now she won't need us anymore. That's all I think about.

June 1946, Andrésy.

It's My Birthday, I'm Nine Years Old

The kids my age are gathered in our room and we've cleaned it and pushed the beds to the sides. They stand in a circle around me singing, "Happy birthday to you...." I'm so proud! The cook has given me two platters, one filled with candies, the other with cookies, and I pass them around. Filled with joy and pride, I move slowly with the two platters, and then, oops! my underwear falls down to the floor and I'm standing there with my bum exposed! All the kids laugh at me. They take away the plates of sweets, and the rest of the kids eat them instead of me. I hate them! Simone, the  counsellor, gets me dressed again, using a diaper pin to hold my rags together. And, poor me, I stand there with my bum covered again and my legs crossed, mourning my stolen happiness.

"Come on, Marguerite! Where's the big girl who turned nine today?" asks Simone. What does she want me to say? I feel deeply humiliated.

Then Nicole holds out the dirty old ball that her brother Frédo found and the miniature Eiffel Tower that Sammy, the eldest one, gave her. "Here, these are for you," she says, hugging me so hard that I can't breathe. And then the others hug me too.

And I surprise myself by saying "Thank you!" and feeling delighted. It seems I'm not the first person this has ever happened to. But on my birthday, it's really too much! From now on, I'll check the elastic.

Tonsils and Adenoids

"Children who get a lot of colds will be operated on by Doctor Pierre," the nurse explains, adding that the doctor is very nice. We will sleep in the infirmary for a week and will have to stay in bed. What a deal!

On the morning of the big day, my heart is pounding wildly, but not with joy. We don't get anything to eat because we need to have an empty stomach to prevent vomiting after the operation. I wait anxiously for my turn. I've never slept in the same room with boys before. They each come back in their underwear, their eyes wide. The nurse puts their pyjamas on as if they were babies.

"Marguerite Élias!" calls a deep voice from the next room.

"That's me." Suddenly not so brave, I go in, trembling. The woman doctor places the ether mask on my face and asks me to count in my head, and the other doctor gives me a shot all the while talking incessantly. I can't understand what he's saying anymore because sleep overcomes me. I wake up shouting with pain as well as fear, it hurts so much. They make me inhale that disagreeable smell again because they need to put me back to sleep to remove my adenoids.

I don't know how I came to be lying in this bed. The boy in the next bed is not in the same class as I am, but one level above. He's lucky, only his nose hurts. For me, the worst thing is swallowing. I can hardly drink and I'm bleeding. They give me ice cubes to suck on. I can't eat, but I'm not hungry anyway. Lucien can never get enough and he takes my share. In exchange, he promises me his hot chocolate. He tells me jokes about the catechism. I can't let myself laugh

– what torture! Then he reads to me from *A Good Little Devil*, which was loaned to me, and it's so sad I could cry. The woman doctor comes and takes our temperatures in our bums, and says we all have the same temperature. Now that we're getting better, we're getting scoldings for making noise late at night. It will all be over tomorrow, when we're going to go back to our dorms. So we're enjoying tonight.

When Mama came with her friend Ary Kaufman, Tamara the counsellor told her I had been courageous. Ary gave me a picture book, as if I didn't know how to read, and I had to say thank you. My mother is expecting a baby in July. And what about me – do I count for anything? Why should I care that he's a musician and that they've moved into a new apartment if I don't live with them?

Henriette is proud because Ary has her rehearse with the choir of the Manoir de Denouval. She's singing the song about the Chinese emperor's nightingale. I'm doing illustrations for the song. Ary plays the organ and the piano in the big hall. I don't know why I have to listen to him since he says I don't have a good ear for music. Without Papa, I feel defenceless.

The Americans

Simone decides what we're wearing and puts ribbons in our hair be-cause the Americans are coming. We mustn't disappoint them. We

greet them filled with hope and they give gifts to the kids who don't
have any family. There's a good reason we sing our hearts out welcoming them – even if they say I sing off-key. Women wearing lots
of jewellery have been kissing me. All afternoon, they've hardly said
anything to me except to ask my name and tell me that it's adorable.
These Americans could take away some kids whose names are on a
list, which makes me feel terrible because my friends could go away
to America. I'd miss them. But my mother promised she wouldn't
leave me here. At the end of the day, a photographer has us pose.
Against my wishes, I have to lend my doll to Maddie. I'm at the top,
standing on a bench, and the photographer calls, "Smile now!" so that
it will be a good picture.

Marc Chagall

Today we have some important visitors. We're all happy because we're
going to have an excellent dinner. We've decorated the dining room.
To welcome our guests, we sing at the top of our lungs, "We love life,
we love love, we love the night, we love the day...," and the celebra-
tion begins. After a speech, we go to our usual places. The tables look

beautiful covered with white sheets. I wait impatiently for this meal; the smells have whetted my appetite. The youngest girl presents flowers to our guest of honour, the painter Marc Chagall.

As a kind of prayer of thanks before the feast, we sing, "Around a table with good friends, how nice to be together," and at the end of the meal, "Thank you for your company, and for the food that we have eaten." Then the older kids clear the tables, the middle ones line up the benches, and the youngest, including me, sit down on the floor. They say thank you to the children and then three gentlemen tell jokes. I love the one about the liar... A father tells his son, "When I was your age, I was the best behaved and the best student in my class," and a mechanical hand comes out and hits him. The hand hits him every time he doesn't tell the truth and he keeps getting hit. The kids roar with laughter and clap like crazy. When the show is over, we go out in front to have our picture taken again and we join hands and form a circle to sing, "If all the children of the world," and the farewell song, the French version of "Auld Lang Syne" – "This is not goodbye, my brothers, we'll see each other again." And in my head, in vain, I'm hoping and saying, "That was not goodbye, my father... yes, Papa, we'll see each other again."

Maxime's Accident

We're doing our homework in the big hall when we hear a loud crash like a rock falling from the sky and the sound of breaking glass. Maxime has fallen into our room from the floor above, making a hole in the glass ceiling. Everyone jumps up. We timidly approach him. He's wearing roller skates and he's bleeding. He repeats, "Mama! Mama!" forgetting that he has no mother anymore.

On the floor above, people are trying to repair and cover the hole made in the glass ceiling. Meanwhile, downstairs, we form a circle around Maxime, looking at him with our mouths open. He seems to be in unbearable pain. The doctor rushes in to take care of him. Tamara is wonderful, she holds him and comforts him. A counsellor comes. Gilbert comes too, carrying his stupid skates. "Is he going to die?" he asks in tears.

But the counsellors have something to say to him. "Bad boy! You both knew you were not allowed to roller skate in the bedrooms! Especially in that one where the floor is made of glass! Let that be a lesson to you!" Without the support of his friend Maxime, poor Gilbert is ashamed and at a loss for words to defend himself. "You're going to be punished," they admonish him. In deathly silence, we leave the room. Finally, the ambulance arrives noisily. We're pushed aside and the ambulance attendants come in the main entrance with their stretcher. Five minutes later, they carry our schoolmate out. The rest of us disperse.

What a lesson for the two boys!

My Chocolate Castle

For a while now, my sister has been in a good mood. When we're given a piece of chocolate for our four o'clock snack, Henriette comes and sits on my bench for a few minutes. I like it when she comes to see me and look forward to it. She whispers in my ear, telling me what she wants. I see my friends Maddie and Charlotte also talking to each other. Henriette comes very close to me and I slip my chocolate into her pocket. Then, as if nothing had happened, she goes back to her place with her friends, who are still talking to each other while looking at me out of the corners of their eyes. I look back at them defiantly. Henriette is going to put my piece of chocolate with the other ones I've given her. I make do with dry bread to satisfy my hunger.

With my head buried under the covers, I see my pieces of chocolate piled up like bricks in a wall that's getting higher and higher.

My plan is to build a castle out of chocolate. When we go back home, there will be chocolate everywhere in my bedroom. I'm so eager for it that I suck on an old candy and finally fall asleep with my mouth full of the taste of sugar while my head is filled with chocolate.

But the liar has once again made a fool of me. "It's a trick so she can give chocolate to her friends," a girl from her dorm informs me, who doesn't like seeing Henriette do this. I feel cheated and sheepish. Even if I tell Mama about it, I'll never get my chocolate back.

My delicious castle melts in front of my eyes and I'm devastated. Now that I refuse to give her my chocolate, she completely ignores me. But she can't take advantage of my gullibility anymore because I no longer trust her.

I Want My Room

I want my own room all to myself at home in Paris, with Choukette at the foot of my bed. I want all this to be over. I want Papa to come back and take me with him. I want my old toys and everything that

belonged to me, everything that was taken from me, that they promised to give me back too long ago. I want my parents, the two of them together. I want to go back for good. That's what I want, God! Do you understand me? If so, show me, and I'll believe in you. All I think about is going back. The baby will soon be born and maybe Mama will write us for once to tell us. She agrees with my choice of Daniel for the middle name, or Danielle if it's a girl. But I'd prefer a boy – one sister is enough for me.

Benoît Daniel was born on July 21, 1946, and Mama and Ary are proud of their son.

Tarnos

For the summer vacation, we're going to a health camp in Tarnos, in the Landes. Mama had running shoes, shorts and other summer clothes sent to us as if she were dead to her daughters. We've packed them in our suitcases along with all the sweets she sent. In the train, I hear someone shout, "Heil Hitler! The pig is dead!" I look out the window and there are German prisoners walking with their hands on their heads. Now Papa can come home. I'm smiling again.

Not far from our camp there was a terrible fire that burned down a good part of the forest in the Landes. It seems there's never been anything like it here before. Everyone formed a huge chain with their buckets and pitchers. We passed pots full of water from hand to hand. The firemen sprayed it with their hoses, but it was in vain. The camp prepared food for the people fighting the fire. They all seemed nice, like friends. After several days, we managed to put it out. Our blue sky has come back, with the sun – and the end of summer. But I did succeed in becoming the champion at *pichenette*, a game where one has to show great dexterity doing tricks with a pocket knife. I threw the knife over my head exactly right and won against some more experienced players. And I broke the record!

I Go Back to Cité Voltaire

Monsieur Ary is waiting for us on the platform. Where's Mama? I had imagined a different welcome, but I'll act as if it's fine until we get back to rue de Charonne. But no, we'll be living on rue Oberkampf, in his house, on the third floor, next door to his sister Hélène. I'm already upset.

Henriette and I share the couch and every time she moves, the back falls on my head. We've seen Choukette, but they haven't given her back to me. Mama is unreachable; she's breastfeeding her baby and working from early morning to late at night. Benoît is adorable, always smiling, never grumpy, a real little doll.

School has started again, but I couldn't stand Saint-Bernard school. It gave me nightmares. I begged my mother and she got Cité Voltaire to accept me. I have to take the métro and get off at Boulets, but it doesn't matter because I would have been too uncomfortable in the other school. I remember all too well what happened before we left Paris. I'm two years behind the other kids my age. My teacher is Madame Stordeur, who has a son my age. He sometimes comes to see us. I'm working seriously, as I promised. But it's discouraging being among the last in the class and instead of being eight like my classmates, I'm ten. I need my father to help me catch up. No, I'm not happy. "Things won't be as they were before," says my mother, "You'll have to resign yourself to it." It's as if Papa had never existed. "You have to forget the past and go forward – it's the present that counts," says Ary, taking me to see the teacher. He makes me feel ashamed when I see him leaning against the wall talking to her. I try to be nice to him, but could he not say I'm his daughter. He likes Henriette better, anyway. She's allowed to play the piano at his sister's, in their knitting workshop behind our bedroom, where I can hear them.

My big sister takes music classes every Thursday while I go to the youth club in passage Charles-Dallery. I'm learning Yiddish with Madame Slovès and I'm enjoying it. The parents of a young man

who was killed during the war gave each of us a pullover and had us pose for a picture. At the festival at the Salle Pleyel, I was dressed as a mouse and sang a song about cats. Everyone clapped for me, even Monsieur Ary.

During the week, my mother teaches her musician the furrier trade and she's tired when she gets home. And on Saturday nights, they go together to their Jewish People's Choir on rue de Paradis. I babysit my little brother and cry along with him. I hold him in my arms and walk up and down in the room that, I don't know why, smells of ether. They can't forbid me to think about Papa, but I'm giving up hope of his coming back. I hear again his pleas to the policemen and their mocking replies. I would like to cry out, but to whom? I put the baby down in his bed – he's Benoît to them, but Daniel to me. And I go to the window and look out at the city where I was born, searching for an answer. But there is none.

My Cousin Goldalé

We went to the hospital to see our cousin Goldalé, whom I didn't know. She doesn't speak much French. She was living in Lithuania with her parents when the Germans occupied it. She was a young teenager, like my friend Hélène Weinstein. Her twin sister and her mother were killed in the gas chambers – the so-called disinfection chambers – a short time after their arrival in the camps. Goldalé was angry at being separated from them, but now she's grateful. She's sixteen now but looks older because people aged quickly in the camps. When I kiss her swollen cheeks, I feel her soft, fine skin. When I touch her, she leans toward me and looks at me lovingly. She's hoping to be able to immigrate to Palestine and find her older sister, Adina, and little brother, Schlomo. She speaks slowly and we listen without interrupting. She has come from Cyprus and Uncle Léon has invited her to stay with him while she waits for permission to take the boat, but she's eager to go. She survived Auschwitz because, against her wishes, her parents cleverly added a year to her age and ordered her to work until she could be saved from that hell. One day, behind the barbed wire, she met her father – my father's brother – who was very emaciated. He begged her to eat everything she could find – even grass! Shortly after, she learned that he had been gassed and then incinerated, like the millions of men, women and children in the huge common graves where my father's ashes would also be. She insists that there's no use crying. She told us that when she heard the people who brought the food in the morning reach the door, she held out not only her hand but also the hand of her dead neighbour to get her portion of bread and soup as well. I can't get over it! At the end, unable to walk by herself without falling, she would give the food to the woman who helped her line up for the roll call. "You can't imagine that place, Rachel," she told my mother with a wail.

I've seen so many sick and wounded people, so many pictures in the papers and in the news at the movies that I can't stop think-ing about them. The corpses are everywhere, as thin as sticks in their striped pyjamas. I refuse to imagine Papa as one of an anonymous crowd of naked people going into the "shower" to be assassinated before being thrown into the crematory oven. I can't accept that they treated him worse than an animal in a slaughterhouse. "At least Raphaël died fighting at Stalingrad," Mama says of her younger brother, half proud and half sad. He was a captain in the Soviet army. She made this gruesome discovery just before giving birth to Benoît Daniel at the Rothschild Hospital.

I fall asleep thinking of Goldalé, her sister, her parents, my two grandmothers and everyone in my family who died – uncles, aunts, paternal grandfather, cousins and especially the one I adore above anyone in the world, my Papa. He doesn't even have a grave I can go to.

I look down from the landing and see him at the bottom of the stairs. Why doesn't he come up? He can't. He has no legs and only one arm. He looks at me sadly from his wheelchair, wearing his old dressing gown. I want to go down and get him, but how will I be able to get him upstairs? I cry hopelessly, "Mama! Mama!"

"Shhhhh. Shhhhh. You're having a nightmare, Marguerite! You'll wake the little one. Calm down and go to sleep now." And she throws herself into the bed where I hear her lover snoring. I block my ears and push my pain down into the deepest part of myself, but I can't make it go away.

Epilogue

I've been protected and helped by a star in the heavens – that of my father.

Between the ages of ten and thirteen, whenever I was not in school, I would go to the communist youth club of the Union des juifs pour las résistance et l'entraide (UJRE; the Union of Jews for Assistance and Resistance), where I learned Yiddish, among other things.

But when I was fourteen, my mother sent me to a summer camp run by another youth organization, the Borochov Dror. They were socialist Zionists for whom Hebrew rather than Yiddish was the language to learn. I was sent there because my mother could not afford any other camp. However, after the camp was over, I decided to join that movement, which had its quarters above the Bataclan movie theatre and was close to my new home, rue Oberkampf. We had in fact moved to my stepfather's former home, which he had finally managed to get back. Leaving the UJRE for the Borochov Dror allowed me to distance myself from my communist stepfather who was active in the party – before and after the war, he had been a volunteer director of the (communist) Jewish People's Choir of Paris.

It was at that time that my sixteen-year-old sister, who was a "cadet" at the UJRE, became pregnant. She had been deprived of love and attention and her equally young partner was an orphan whose parents had both been murdered in a death camp. My sister was sent to a convent for unwed pregnant girls near the Alésia métro station. During those six months, I went to visit her regularly, in spite of the shame I felt. Seven days after her beautiful baby daughter was born, my sister had to give her up for adoption as she had no support and no money to keep her. I did get to hold her baby girl in my arms before she was taken away. The secret of her baby was the heaviest I had to carry. It was only in July of 2006 that I revealed it to her son, at his behest, because he wanted to understand why his mother had suffered such mental distress at the end of her life.

At fourteen years old, I received an unexpected gift – a first prize in drawing – that enabled me to enroll in Élisa-Lemonnier technical college. But family and financial problems prevented me from finishing my third year there. I then worked as a temporary telephone operator and later as a temp worker, sorting mail at the Postes, Télégrammes et Téléphones. I kept attending meetings at the Borochov Dror and I eventually became a volunteer counsellor when I turned sixteen.

Often, on Sunday mornings, I would collect money from the Jewish families on my list for the benefit of the Keren Kayemeth LeIsrael (the Jewish National Fund), which planted trees in the land of our ancestors. On Sunday afternoons, we would sometimes gather the Jewish children playing in the streets of our neighbourhoods and take them to have fun and share their meagre "goûters" (the traditional five o'clock snacks) in the Bois de Vincennes and other places.

At eighteen, I became a paymistress on contract at the army's administrative and accounting centre in Pantin, where I calculated the monthly pay and benefits for four hundred soldiers. I held that job for five years but my contracts had to be renewed every six months and I had no hope of advancement because I had never graduated from high school. I had also thought of making *aliyah* to Israel to work on a kibbutz, but since I was not yet twenty-one and still a minor, Mama was able to prevent me from leaving the country. Then I worked for her in her old business until 1967 and gave her moral support until the end of her life in 1996, in spite of everything.

In July 1962, at the age of twenty-six, I had the good luck to meet the Bengali engineer who changed my life. We managed to marry in April 1965, while he was doing his doctorate in chemical engineering at the École Centrale in Paris. In 1967, the offer of a teaching position at the University of British Columbia, in Vancouver, brought us to Canada. In 1969, the birth of our son gave us the joy and pride of parenthood, and in September of that year my husband was offered a position at Laval University in Québec, which brought us a bit closer to Paris. In 1971, we moved to Longueuil when a new position as a professor of chemistry opened for my husband there.

In 1976, after a law passed requiring the children of immigrants to Québec to be educated in French, I became a volunteer, helping these children in the English-language schools attended by our son, and thus came out of my isolation. I was in turn an academic assistant in French, a counsellor for younger children, an assistant for children with difficulties and a self-taught drawing teacher, with no remuneration other than the knowledge that I was useful.

In 1990, timidly, I undertook to write this book. I was unable to write the painful passages and our son suggested that I illustrate them and then organize them in chronological order. Once that was done, I was able to finish the text.

In my house in Canada, where I finally feel at home, I still live with the dead in my family. In my nightmares, I see Papa – younger than I am now – skeletal, shaven and naked, on the path to a crematorium, a terrible image that continues to haunt me.

During the long winter nights, I go over my memories and feel sad at being so far from some of my dearest friends and family. But, in the morning, if the sun is shining, I open my window and think of those I so unjustly lost as I breathe in the happiness of freedom in this great country we have chosen.

Appendix

Author's note

All the proper names in this book are authentic with the exception of those of the teacher Madame Petit, Yvette and Madame Martin. My sister's name has been slightly modified in order to spare myself a painful confrontation.

The message from our concierge, reproduced on page 32, is only one example of her many attempts to profit financially from our precarious situation. To avoid her constant surveillance, our faithful clients had to come to us at night through the neighbouring bistro, whose door was next to ours.

The hand I have drawn on page 13 is not that of Mademoiselle Aubertin, but my own. As for the delicious chocolates in it, they are the fruit of my greedy imagination.

Pelleteries en Gros

LÉONCE TOURNE

RUE DU FAUB POISSONNIERE

PARIS 9

LONDRES
NEW-YORK

, 27 Juin

Monsieur E L I A S H

99 Rue de Charonne

P A R I S

artisan en fourrures et continuer à être inscrit au
Registre des Métiers, et dans les limites restrictives
imposées par les Ordonnances des Autorités d'Occupation.

Je vous précise notamment que vous ne devez
avoir ni boutique, ni enseigne, ni stock, ni clientèle
particulière. Vous devez travailler uniquement à façon
pour le compte de maisons de fourrures, et vous voudrez
bien m'adresser les attestations des entreprises pour
le compte desquelles vous travaillez.

Je crois utile de vous souligner les graves
responsabilités personnelles que vous pourriez encourir
si vous contreveniez à ces prescriptions.

Veuillez agréer, Monsieur, l'assurance de mes
sentiments distingués.

The letter of warning sent by the administrator of my father's business appointed by the Vichy administration, Léonce Tourne:

Wholesale Furs
Léonce Tourne
Rue du Faubourg Poissonnière

June 27, 1941

Mr. ÉLIASH
99 Rue de Charonne

This letter is to inform you that you can remain an independent furrier and be registered as a member of the Trades Association only within the restrictions imposed by the ordinances of the Occupying Authority.

In particular, I want to notify you that you cannot own a store, nor can you have any signage, stock or personal clients. You are <u>only allowed to do contract work</u> for other furriers. Please make sure you send me the necessary certificates from the companies you do work for.

I should remind you that you would suffer great personal consequences were you to contravene these orders.

Sincerely,

[signature]

Ateliers de DRANCY

Bâtiment du 99, rue de Charonne

A letter from our landlord, Monsieur Gellé, dated July 10, 1941. Looking at the letterhead, I discovered a terrible coincidence: beside the photograph of our building, there is a photograph of another factory belonging to Monsieur Gellé, in Drancy – the very place where Papa would be interned and from which our friend in the prefecture, Madame Graziani, would try in vain to have him freed as a veteran and a well-known businessman established in France for sixteen years.

Opening of the Drancy camp

OUVERTURE DU CAMP DE DRANCY

4232 hommes internés à DRANCY, cet ensemble d'HLM inachevé où tout manque

Les autobus les conduisent à DRANCY. Ce sont les raflés qui vont inaugurer ce camp installé à la hâte dans un ensemble d'immeubles HLM inachevés où tout manque : cloisons et toilettes. Des latrines sont installées dans la cour.

**A l'arrivée au camp,
ils sont 4.232 hommes internés,
dont 1500 Français ou naturalisés.
Sur 4232 raflés, plus de 3.200
sont du XIe.**

Four thousand two hundred and thirty-two (4,232) men were interned at Drancy, in an unfinished, low-cost housing complex lacking the most basic amenities.

They were taken to Drancy in buses. The first victims of *rafles* inaugurated the camp, which had been hastily set up in an unfinished, low-cost housing complex that lacked everything, including partitions and toilets. Latrines were installed in the courtyard.

There were 4,232 men picked up and interned at the camp, 1,500 of whom were French-born or naturalized. More than 3,200 of the 4,232 were from the 11th arrondissement.

Dear Marguerite,

I do not want to delve back into our difficult past, but I think that we need to thank you. We have always thought that if my husband was still alive, it is because of your presence in our house at the time of the arrest by the Résistance. There is one thing that made a strong impression on all of us and that is your memory; this thing of yours scares me a bit. You probably remember that I was strict. I did not always understand you. See, Marguerite, you have to excuse and even forgive me. I was only a second-hand mom and I certainly did not

Part of Madame Chatenay's answer to the first letter I sent her, when I had reached adulthood. Unbeknownst to me, my mother had cut this passage out of the letter.

Glossary

aliyah (Hebrew; pl. aliyot, literally, ascent) A term used by Jews and modern Israelis to refer to Jewish immigration to Israel; the term is also used to refer to "going up" to the altar in a synagogue to read from the Torah.

antisemitism Prejudice, discrimination, persecution and/or hatred against Jewish people, institutions, culture and symbols.

armistice *See* Franco-German armistice.

Auschwitz (German; in Polish, Oświęcim) A town in southern Poland approximately forty kilometres from Krakow, it is also the name of the largest complex of Nazi concentration camps that were built nearby. The Auschwitz complex contained three main camps: Auschwitz I, a slave labour camp built in May 1940; Auschwitz II-Birkenau, a death camp built in early 1942; and Auschwitz-Monowitz, a slave labour camp built in October 1942. In 1941, Auschwitz I was a testing site for usage of the lethal gas Zyklon B as a method of mass killing, which then went into wide usage. Between 1942 and 1944, approximately 70,000 French Jews were deported to Auschwitz, where an estimated 1.1 million people were murdered. Approximately 950,000 of the people killed were Jewish; 74,000 Polish; 21,000 Roma; 15,000 Soviet prisoners of war; and 10,000–15,000 other nationalities. The Auschwitz complex was liberated by the Soviet army in January 1945. *See also* Nazi camps.

Boches (French) A derogatory term used during both world wars to refer to Germans.

Borochov Dror A socialist Zionist youth group based on the ideas of Ber Borochov (1881–1917), a Marxist Zionist theorist who was one of the founders of the Labour Zionist movement. *See also* Zionism.

British Mandate Palestine The area of the Middle East under British rule from 1923 to 1948, as established by the League of Nations after World War I. During that time, the United Kingdom severely restricted Jewish immigration. The Mandate area encompassed present-day Israel, Jordan, the West Bank and the Gaza Strip.

Chagall, Marc (1887–1985) An artist of Russian-Jewish descent who was famous for his paintings and stained glass windows.

Compiègne A municipality in northern France about seventy kilometres from Paris that was the site of the Royallieu internment and transit camp after the German occupation of France in 1940. By June 1941 the camp was under Nazi control and held Soviet prisoners of war, after which it held Jews and political prisoners such as communists and members of resistance groups. In February 1942, a separate camp for Jews was established. Between 1941 and 1944, between 40,000 and 45,000 prisoners passed through the camp, from where they were deported to Auschwitz and other Nazi camps.

Cyprus An island nation in the Mediterranean and former British colony that was granted independence from Great Britain in 1960. In the 1940s, Cyprus was the location of British detention camps for European Jewish refugees who were attempting to illegally immigrate to British Mandate Palestine. More than 50,000 Jewish refugees were interned in these camps. *See also* British Mandate Palestine.

de Gaulle, Charles André Joseph Marie (1890–1970) French general and statesman who opposed both the Nazi regime and the French collaborationist Vichy government. De Gaulle, a World War I veteran and Brigadier General in World War II, escaped to London after the fall of France in 1940. In London, de Gaulle organized the Free French Forces, a partisan and resistance group comprised of French officers in exile. After the war, de Gaulle served as head of the French provisional government from 1944 to 1946, and as president of France from 1958 to 1969.

demarcation line The boundary between the northern part of France occupied by the Germans (Occupied Zone) and the southern Unoccupied Zone that was under the control of the Vichy government. *See also* Free zone; Vichy.

Drancy A northeastern suburb of Paris that was the site of an internment and transit camp from which about 65,000 people, almost all Jews, were deported to concentration and death camps. The camp was established in August 1941 and was run by the French police until July 1943, when the Nazi SS took it over until its liberation in August 1944.

Exode The mass exodus of millions of French civilians between the end of May and mid-June 1940 as German troops neared the city of Paris.

Franco-German armistice The agreement signed between Nazi Germany and France on June 22, 1940 that established a German occupation zone in northern France and a French-administered zone, also known as the "Free zone" in southern France. *See also* Free zone; Vichy.

Free zone (in French, *Zone libre*) The southern region of France that was under nominal French sovereignty between June 1940 and November 1942, after which it was occupied by Germany. *See also* Vichy.

French Forces of the Interior (FFI) The formal name given to the French rural and urban resistance fighters after the Normandy landings on June 6, 1944. In June 1944, the forces were comprised of approximately 100,000; by October of that year the numbers had grown to 400,000. *See also Maquis; Résistance.*

Garel circuit The underground network in Paris named after one of its organizers, George Garel, who helped rescue Jewish children from transit camps and provided them with false identification papers and refuge with Christian families. The Garel circuit, which began operating mid-1942, was affiliated with the OSE (Œuvre de secours aux enfants) and saved more than one thousand children. *See also* OSE (Œuvre de secours aux enfants).

Keren Kayemeth LeIsrael (Hebrew; in English, Jewish National Fund) A non-profit organization founded in 1901 to buy, lease and develop the land of pre-state Israel. The Jewish National Fund's projects currently include water conservation, land development and planting trees, of which more than 240 million have been planted since its inception.

kibbutz (Hebrew) A collectively owned farm or settlement in Israel democratically governed by its members.

Lord's Prayer (in Latin, Oratio Dominica, also called Pater Noster, "Our Father") A common prayer in Christian liturgy, it appears in the New Testament in two versions (short and long) as part of the teachings of Jesus and as a model of prayer.

Manoir de Denouval A mansion in Andrésy, France about twenty-five kilometres from Paris that was bought by the Union of Jews for Assistance and Resistance (UJRE) in December 1945 to house and support Jewish war orphans. Between 1945 and 1949, approximately 200 children lived in the mansion. *See also* Union of Jews for Assistance and Resistance.

Maquis (French; abbreviation of *maquisards*; literally, thicket) The term for French resistance fighters in rural areas during World War II. The *Maquis* originated from a group of men, mostly communist and socialist, who fled to mountainous terrain (hence their name, which loosely translates as "bush") to avoid being arrested by the Gestapo in occupied France due to their political orientation. By early 1943, the *Maquis* had grown in strength and organization due to the thousands of new members who were avoiding the new law of conscription in France, the Service du Travail Obligatoire, which led to forced labour in Germany. The *Maquis* at first focused on sabotaging German communication and transport lines as well as providing protection to Jews and refugees, and later were able to organize armed resistance due to British and American support. After the Normandy landings on June 6, 1944, the *Maquis* became formalized into the French Forces of the Interior. *See also* French Forces of the Interior; *Résistance.*

Milice (short form of *Milice française*; French militia) A paramilitary force that operated in France between 1943 and 1944 to counter the French resistance. The *Milice* also helped in rounding up Jews for deportation.

National Revolution The racist, antisemitic ideology of the Vichy regime headed by Maréchal Philippe Pétain. *See also* Pétain, Philippe; Statutes on Jews; Vichy.

Nazi camps The Nazis established roughly 20,000 prison camps between 1933 and 1945. Although the term concentration camp is often used to refer generally to all these facilities, the various camps in fact served a wide variety of functions. They included concentration camps; forced labour camps; prisoner-of-war (POW) camps; transit camps; and death camps. Concentration camps were detention facilities first built in 1933 to imprison "enemies of the state," while forced labour camps held prisoners who had to do hard physical labour under brutal working conditions. POW camps were designated for captured prisoners of war and transit camps operated as holding facilities for Jews who were to be transported to main camps – often death camps in Poland. Death camps were killing centres where designated groups of people were murdered on a highly organized, mass scale. Some camps, such as Mauthausen, combined several of these functions into a huge complex of camps.

OSE (Œuvre de secours aux enfants) (French; Children's Relief Agency) A French-Jewish organization that helped rescue thousands of Jewish refugee children during World War II. The OSE was founded in Russia in 1912 and its offices were relocated to France in 1933, where it set up more than a dozen orphanages and homes; hid children from the Nazis; and, among other underground operations, arranged for their transfer to the US and Switzerland. By March 1942, the OSE, in order to continue its work, was forced under Vichy law to incorporate into the General Union of the Jews of France (UGIF), an organization that collaborated with the Nazis. When Germany occupied the south of France in November 1942, much of OSE's work to rescue children went underground and it increased its efforts to both move children to safer homes in the Italian-occupied southeast and smuggle children across the Swiss border.

Pétain, Philippe (1856–1951) French general and Maréchal (Marshal) of France who was the chief of state of the French government in Vichy from 1940 to 1944. After the war, Pétain was tried for treason for his collaboration with the Nazis and was sentenced to death, which was commuted to life imprisonment. *See also* Vichy.

pogrom (Russian; to wreak havoc, to demolish) A violent attack on a distinct ethnic group. The term most commonly refers to nineteenth- and twentieth- century attacks on Jews in the Russian Empire.

rafle (French) roundup. *See also* Vélodrome d'Hiver.

Résistance The collective term for the French resistance movement during World War II. In rural areas, the group was known as the *Maquis*. The *Résistance* published underground newspapers, helped Allied prisoners-of-war escape, sabotaged German war equipment and created intelligence networks that gathered military information in order to gain armament support from Britain. *See also* Maquis.

SERE (Service d'évacuation et de regroupement des enfants) (French; Office of Evacuation and Regrouping of Children) A resistance organization created between 1942 and 1943 that was affiliated with the OSE (Œuvre de secours aux enfants) and helped to rescue Jewish children, specifically those whose parents had been deported, by establishing them with Christian families. *See also* OSE (Œuvre de secours aux enfants).

"The Song of the Partisans" A resistance song written by Jewish poet and partisan Hersh Glik while he was in the ghetto in Vilnius, Lithuania. The song was an emblem of hope and defiance, and it quickly spread to other prisoners in Nazi camps. It was eventually translated into Hebrew, Polish, Russian, Spanish, Romanian, Dutch and English.

Statutes on Jews The antisemitic legislations enacted by the Vichy regime in 1940 and 1941. The first Statute of October 3, 1940 defined the criteria for being Jewish, excluded Jews from professions such as public and military service and interned foreign Jews in camps. The second Statute expanded the ban on Jewish employment to include all commercial and industrial sectors and confiscated Jewish property. *See also* Vichy.

Union des juifs pour la résistance et l'entraide (UJRE) (French; in English, the Union of Jews for Assistance and Resistance) A Paris-based and communist-led organization that was created in 1943. Originally called Solidarité and established in August 1940 to resist the Nazi occupation, the group first focused on sabotaging German industry and establishing partisan groups; by 1943, it had changed tactics and focused on hiding and protecting Jewish children from deportation.

Vélodrome d'Hiver A sports stadium in Paris that was the site of a major roundup of Jews in France on July 16 and 17, 1942. Approximately 12,000 were arrested and interned in the stadium, from which they were deported to transit camps and, eventually, Nazi death camps.

Vichy A resort town in south-central France that was the seat of the government of Maréchal Pétain in unoccupied France. The Franco-German armistice of June 22, 1940, divided France into two zones: the northern three-fifths to be under German military occupation and the remaining southern region to be under nominal French sovereignty, also referred to as the *Zone libre* ("Free zone"). In October 1940 the administration in Vichy enacted antisemitic legislation, independently of Germany, and later collaborated with Nazi Germany by interning Jews in Drancy, which later led to their deportation to death camps. *See also* Drancy; Pétain, Philippe.

yellow star The six-pointed star, called the Star of David, which is the ancient and most recognizable symbol of Judaism. During World War II, many Jews in Nazi-occupied areas were forced to wear a badge or armband with the Star of David on it as an identifying mark of their lesser status and to single them out as targets for persecution.

Yiddish A language derived from Middle High German with elements of Hebrew, Aramaic, Romance and Slavic languages, and written in Hebrew characters. Spoken by Jews in east-central Europe for roughly a thousand years from the tenth century to the mid-twentieth century, it was still the most common language among European Jews until the outbreak of World War II. There are similarities between Yiddish and contemporary German.

Zionism A movement promoted by the Viennese Jewish journalist Theodor Herzl, who argued in his 1896 book *Der Judenstaat* (The Jewish State) that the best way to resolve the problem of antisemitism and persecution of Jews in Europe was to create an independent Jewish state in the historic Jewish homeland of Biblical Israel. Zionists also promoted the revival of Hebrew as a Jewish national language.

Photographs

1 Marguerite's paternal great-grandfather, Shlomo Éliashev.
2 Shlomo Éliashev's gravestone in the Mount of Olives cemetery, Jerusalem.

1 Marguerite's father, Maurice Élias (Srol Moïse Éliash), circa 1930.
2 Maurice Élias (left) with his brother, Marguerite's Uncle Léon, who had just enrolled in the French army. Paris, circa 1933.

Marguerite (left) and her sister Henriette wearing their rabbit skin fur coats on the mountain at Vatilieu during their time with the Chatenay family. Circa 1943.

1   Marguerite's mother, Rachel Perl Élias (second from the left), with the money-
    lender (left) after the war. Marguerite, far right, is standing beside her brother,
    Benoît. Circa 1948.

2   The card that Marguerite's mother received from the French government in 1954
    identifying her as a war victim whose property had been confiscated and entitling
    her to some form of compensation.

3   Document issued by the Minister of Veterans and War Victims in 1955 con-
    firming the dates of Marguerite's father's internment, deportation and death.

1 Marguerite (third row, second from the right) at eleven years old in the Cité Voltaire public school class photo. Paris, 1947.

2 Thirteen-year-old Marguerite (front, right) in a Yiddish play at summer camp, 1950.

1 Enjoying the socialist Zionist Borochov Dror summer camp, circa 1953. Marguerite is in the front row, far left.

2 The communist Jewish People's choir of Paris. Marguerite's stepfather, Ary Kaufman (second row, third from the left) was the volunteer director. Marguerite's mother is sitting to his left.

1

2

3

1 Henriette, Marguerite's older sister, at seventeen. Paris, 1951.

2 Marguerite, age twenty-two.

3 Marguerite (left side, second desk back) in the payroll department of the army, where she worked between 1954 and 1959.

Marguerite and Abdul Quddus' wedding photo, April 17, 1965. Front row, left to right: Marguerite's mother, Rachel; Abdul; Marguerite; Benoît. Back row, left to right: Marguerite's cousin, Monique Zanditénas; Abdul's cousin, Sha Qureshi; Madame Moireau, a friend and client from before the war; and Marguerite and Abdul's neighbour.

1

2

1 Marguerite and Abdul on the way to Canada on the RMS *Carmania*. Le Havre, August 25, 1967.

2 The young couple in Vancouver, 1968.

1

2

1 & 2 Marguerite volunteering at schools in Montreal in the mid to late 1970s.

1 Dinner party at Benoît's house in Paris. From left to right: Marguerite, Benoît and Henriette. Sitting in front are Marguerite's son, Michael, and her niece, Johanna. 1980.

2 Marguerite and Michael visiting Antoinette and Robert Chatenay. Vatilieu, 1980.

3 Marguerite's nephew, Bruno Massardo (left) with her son, Michael, and grandson, Nicolas. 2012.

Marguerite Élias Quddus, 2012.

Index

The Azrieli Foundation was established in 1989 to realize and extend the philanthropic vision of David J. Azrieli, C.M., C.Q., M.Arch. The Foundation's mission is to support a wide spectrum of initiatives in education and research. The Azrieli Foundation is an active supporter of programs in the fields of Jewish education, the education of architects, scientific and medical research, and education in the arts. The Azrieli Foundation's many well-known initiatives include: the Holocaust Survivor Memoirs Program, which collects, preserves, publishes and distributes the written memoirs of survivors in Canada; the Azrieli Institute for Educational Empowerment, an innovative program successfully working to keep at-risk youth in school; and the Azrieli Fellows Program, which promotes academic excellence and leadership on the graduate level at Israeli universities.